# the dog care handbook

# the dog care handbook

**THE COMPLETE GUIDE
FOR A HEALTHY, HAPPY
AND WELL-TRAINED DOG**

## Sophie Collins

Quercus

# Contents

# Introduction

Fifty years ago a book like this one would have had large sections on obedience training, while the rest – rather basic by contemporary standards – would have simply covered the feeding and healthcare of dogs. Over the last few decades, however, a huge amount of research and great advances in our understanding of dog behaviour have resulted in a revolution in the treatment and training of our pets. These days, pet dogs are more likely to be perceived as individuals and to be trained by methods that aren't reliant on punishment but that work with dogs' own understanding and motivation in a way that would have been unheard of just half a century ago.

That dogs are descended from wolves is well known (in fact, the DNA of dogs and wolves is so close that they are counted as a single species by naturalists); what's less appreciated, perhaps, is the extraordinary degree of adaptation which domestic dogs have achieved since they stopped being wolves. It's often noted that dogs live in a human world, but if you take a minute to think about what that actually means you realize what an achievement it is.

Dogs don't understand our language (they can be taught to link specific words with specific objects or actions, but that isn't the same thing) and our bodies are so different from theirs that our body language must be quite mysterious to them – in fact, our behaviour generally is

probably inexplicable for a large part of the time.
Furthermore, our world is set up around language,
while theirs is based around their senses – most particularly their
sense of smell. Yet our world is set up to suit us and basically dogs are
just expected to fit in. And that so many dogs have managed this, with
enthusiasm and good grace, goes a long way to explaining why many
people hold their pets in such high regard and lavish them with so
much love and affection.

To enjoy the full benefit of a canine/human relationship, it's worth
learning the basics of dog behaviour – at least enough to read the
strongest signals your dog sends you, telling you that he's happy, afraid,
apprehensive or angry. The first chapter on dog behaviour covers some
canine body language. The signals that dogs send us and one another
can be far more subtle than you'd think, and you'll miss a lot of them
unless you know what to look for. It also gives some ideas about ways
you can communicate with your dog on his own terms rather than
relying on him to interpret, and then act on, yours.

Picking the right dog – the perfect match in terms of temperament,
energy levels, size, and grooming and feeding requirements – is probably
the single most important aspect of pet ownership. If you don't get that
part right, you may never achieve the enjoyable, evenly balanced
relationship between dog and owner that most people strive for, so the
second chapter, on choosing a dog, takes you through all the questions

you need to ask, both of yourself and other people, to make sure that you choose the best dog for you in the first place. Puppy or adult, pedigree or rescue dog, you will be able to find all the information you need to send you in the right direction.

If you're a dog novice, you'll want to know what you need to do during the first few days and weeks with your new pet and how to care for him, from picking the right diet to starting out on the right foot in terms of training and discipline. Basic dog care, the third chapter, looks at what to do with the new arrival from the very first day, whether you're bringing home a tiny puppy or an adult rescue dog. You'll learn the sensible way to introduce your dog to new experiences and to deal with problems when things don't go quite as you hoped, as well as learning the basics of feeding and grooming that you'll be following every day of your dog's life.

Having made sure your pet's settled at home, we address the question of training – how to turn the dog you've got into the dog you want. We look at the rules of canine good citizenship and at how to get your dog to understand what you want and to establish yourself as a benevolent leader who deserves to be followed, rather than a domestic despot who doesn't command your dog's respect. From the essential (walking to heel, learning to stay) to the optional but fun (teaching tricks), this fourth chapter guides you through the whole process of basic training and deals with the problems that may arise along the way. And, whatever your dog's energy levels, it looks at exercise, too, and at how much is enough (it's almost always more than you think). Dogs have been credited with turning even confirmed couch potatoes into enthusiastic walkers, so you too benefit from giving your best friend what he needs.

The book's final chapter, on keeping your dog healthy, goes into the essentials of pet care and all the many health options now available. Whether it's simple advice on finding the best veterinarian or the basics of pest control, you'll find it covered, but we also look at the many alternative treatments and therapies, from chiropractic medicine to homeopathy, that are now offered for pets. And, lastly, you'll learn how to care for your pet up to his very last day and how to deal with the fact (which we know but which to the owners of elderly dogs can sometimes seem hardly bearable) that the chances are that he will die before you do.

Whether you start at the beginning and read through to the end – in which case you'll have given yourself a solid course on what you need to know to be a good dog owner – or use it as a dip-in reference, this book contains all the up-to-date information you need both to find the right dog, and to care for him when you do.

# Dog behaviour

Dogs have integrated themselves into our everyday lives so skilfully that it's easy to recognize human emotions in many of their behaviours and we can make the mistake of thinking they are just like us. Learning to interpret canine behaviour on its own terms, by understanding how and why dogs behave in the wild and in modern, domestic settings, will bring you more rewarding results as a dog owner.

In the past it was widely believed that pack mentality within wolf and wild dog communities was based on 'aggressive' and 'submissive' personalities. However, recent research shows that dogs are skilled negotiators, and that pack members take on different roles, depending on the tasks in hand, and their individual personalities and strengths.

These recent studies have influenced theories on training and how best to incorporate dogs into our households as pets. This chapter looks at the history of dogs, at characteristic dog behaviour, and at how to 'dogwatch' and interpret your pet's body language.

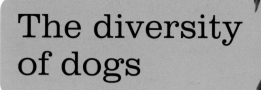

# The diversity of dogs

All 'tame' dogs belong to one mammalian species – *Canis familiaris*. But, from the German shepherd to the Chihuahua, the pug to the Great Dane, an extraordinary diversity has grown up that makes them appear to be dozens of different species.

Left to themselves for 20 generations, without human intervention, a group of a dozen or so different breeds of domestic dog would crossbreed and create a new generation of more or less generic appearance. Gone would be the wide range of outward characteristics we appreciate in our pets today. These crossbred dogs would probably weigh around 16 to 18 kilograms (35 to 40 lb), they would be mostly tan in colour and they would have the balanced, solid-waisted silhouette that is still characteristic of many practical working breeds, such as Border collies. Down the centuries, dogs have been developed from their earlier selves to the point at which many breeds are hardly recognizable as the animal that was indispensable to early hunter-gatherers.

## DOMESTIC DOGS

Dogs have been sharing the lives of humans for thousands of years. The first dogs welcomed as useful companions probably looked like our generic canine: lean and fit, neat, fast and largely capable of fending for themselves.

It's not known whether, as originally thought, dogs are direct descendants from wolves, or if the two species share an early canid as a common ancestor. Other contemporary canine relatives

Left: **Like other mammals, dogs feed their litters with milk. Puppies can't usually fend for themselves until they are at least four or five months old.**

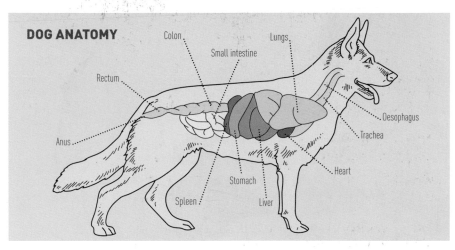

## DOG ANATOMY

Colon · · · Lungs · · ·

Small intestine

Rectum · · ·

· · · Oesophagus

· · · Trachea

Anus · · · · · · ·

· · · Heart

Stomach

Spleen · · · Liver

include jackals, coyotes and dingoes, as well as the African and Asian wild dogs. Behaviourists point out that, while they share much instinctive behaviour with dogs, wolves seem to grow out of many doglike attributes. To look at it the other way around, grown dogs behave more like juvenile wolves than like adult ones.

The domestication of dogs seems to have encouraged neotony in the species – a process whereby the adults retain many of the characteristics of juveniles, both physical and behavioural, all their lives. Examples of this would be the floppy ears seen in many domestic dog breeds (and in wolf cubs, but never in an adult wolf), and the fact that dogs play all their lives, rather than just in puppyhood.

Quite why it has been possible to breed dogs so variously isn't known, and the dog is the only species with this characteristic. Cats, for example, bred for hundreds of years for specific looks and character, remain far more immediately identifiable as cats.

## BASIC INSTINCT **Canine specialists**

Perhaps the most astonishing thing about the domestic dog is the sheer range of specialist jobs which it can be trained to do. Dogs have been bred specifically to hunt various species, including wolves, lions, boars and badgers, as well as to accompany horse-drawn carriages, and to lounge in the laps of royalty. The prize for sheer oddness of role might be taken by the Nova Scotia duck tolling retriever, trained to frolic in the shallow waters at the edge of a lake and attract the attention of the local ducks which, when their defences were down, could then be picked off by the dog's owner.

# Dogs in the wild

In the past, dogs were widely believed to be no more nor less than tamed wolves. Today, their origins are seen as rather more complicated. There are a number of unanswered questions concerning the history of canine–human relations.

## WILD VS DOMESTIC

Many people refer to feral dogs as wild dogs. They are, in fact, stray and freely breeding examples of *Canis familiaris*, which have no owners and live around settlements, whether in the Third World or in highly developed cities, scavenging and using their wits to survive. The true remaining wild members of the dog family are a different species from these dogs (which are the ones we keep as pets). Wild dogs include the Australian dingo, the dhole (known as the wild dog of Asia) and *Lycaon*

*pictus*, the wild dog of Africa, which literally means 'painted wolf', as well as the coyote and the jackal.

Although domestic dogs share virtually identical DNA with wolves (to the extent that scientifically they are treated as the same species), behaviourally they are very different. Students of species development now believe that it is likely that there was an intervening developmental stage between wild wolf and tame dog.

They think the companion dogs we keep as pets today descended through a semi-feral dog that gradually became dependent on human settlements, first for its food and, after it had proved its use as a guard, ultimately for its shelter too. Nevertheless, the behaviour of true wild dogs still helps us understand the hardwiring of domestic dogs. The body language of our pets, in particular, remains in many ways similar to that of their wild cousins.

Left: **Like other wild dogs, the dhole or wild dog of Asia is a different species to the dogs that we keep as pets or that have become stray or 'feral' dogs.**

Above: **Many wild dogs, like dingos, live in packs consisting of an extended family, often with one breeding couple at their centre.**

## LIVING SOCIALLY

Living as part of a social group invariably calls for complex behaviour. There's an enduring and mistaken idea that life in the wild must involve a lot of fighting. Most dog owners are familiar with the concept of an alpha dog, and it used to be thought that such dogs would only keep their positions by tooth-and-claw conflict and constant 'proving' of their status to those pack members on lower social rungs.

Actually, living in the wild is too demanding and involves too many outside pressures to allow for much in-pack conflict. Students of dog behaviour have generally concluded that the status quo within any pack is kept in place with much subtler and more nuanced behaviour. The old saying, 'dog eat dog', is far from accurate. In fact, research on the African wild dog has revealed that the puppies and the elderly within the pack are actively cared for by fitter and more able pack members, while studies of wolf packs have revealed a complicated and highly cooperative society, within which different roles are performed by whichever member of the pack is deemed best suited to them.

## ESTABLISHING RANK

This doesn't mean that there isn't any jockeying for position in wild dog packs, rather that ways of sorting out comparative status have evolved to enable individual animals to find their role without the necessity for damaging displays of brute force.

In reality, the majority of canine disagreements take place between middle-ranking members of the pack. The lowest and the highest ranking generally seem to accept where they belong in the social pecking order.

# Living in a pack

What can we learn about pets from looking at social interaction between canines that live together? As social animals, dogs are very adept at conducting themselves within a human context, but just as people are always people, dogs are always dogs.

Experienced trainers as well as behaviourists look at how we can make ourselves understood by dogs, as well as how we can learn to read their behaviour. Learning to do both gives us the best chance of having a pet that is happy and understands what is wanted from him – because we've learned to speak enough 'dog' to be able to let him know.

## FIXING STATUS

So-called 'alpha' dogs are natural leaders. They're assertive and calm; if they were people, they could be said to have good management skills. Alpha dogs can deal with the pretensions of a wannabe dog quickly and straightforwardly, with a display of strength, or simply with confident behaviour. They don't doubt themselves, so lower ranking dogs don't doubt them either. When dog trainers talk about owners needing to provide leadership, this is the kind of leadership they mean: unambiguous, strong and easy to read.

In a pack, any fighting tends to involve dogs who aspire to leadership but who don't have the natural confidence to deliver it. If your pet sometimes lacks confidence but is nonetheless highly status conscious, you need to be especially sure to be both firm and consistent in order to maintain your benevolent leadership role. Not all dogs are so status-aware – some, in fact, seem to be almost indifferent to status, and these are the characters who, in an all-dog society, might occupy fairly lowly roles without minding, or ever aspiring to improve their rank. How status-aware any dog is depends as much on his own personality as

## BASIC INSTINCT **Anxiety**

Anxiety in dogs, whether it's caused by status worries or not, is most effectively quelled by a clear, firm and kindly regime. There's some evidence that less confident dogs reach a peak of anxiety if they feel that they 'need' to manage things. If they aren't given the option, they are more able to relax.

anything else. We've all encountered mellow, easygoing pets, who simply walk away from trouble, clearly opting out of any situations that might lead to conflict.

Both in the pack and in the home, the toughest dog to manage is probably the dog who has a very developed awareness of status combined with an anxiety about his own position in the ranks. His lack of confidence is likely to lead him to jockey for position and to push his luck (both with you, his owner and with other dogs).

If he was out in a pack, which has to find its own food and manage its own survival, he would be likely to have less chance to develop too much anxiety over status because the animals simply don't have enough time to devote to it.

Right: **Wolves and dogs in the wild don't spend much time in-fighting – the business of survival is too tough to allow for it. Instead, status is decided by subtler means, such as the use of confident body language.**

Above: **On guard. The guarding instinct, still powerful in the majority of domestic dogs, is particularly developed around valued resources: food, home (the 'den') and, for many pets, toys.**

In a domestic situation, though, the tame relative of these wild dogs may need to be kept occupied by the team leader – their owner – to ensure that he doesn't start to become over-concerned with who is top dog.

## GROWING UP

In dog society, a puppy is socialized naturally by the canine community, by both the adults and its fellow puppies. Discipline is given first by the puppy's mother, then by other adults, all of whom will correct a puppy, sometimes forcefully, for rude or pushy behaviour.

The correction can look rather brutal to human eyes – the adult dog may growl, lunge and snap – but puppies are very rarely damaged or even bitten in these encounters, however much noise (and it can be considerable) that the adult chooses to make. In addition, the presence of other young in the litter ensures that every puppy has to share resources – food, and any natural playthings – so that puppies learn to tolerate frustrations and setbacks, and take in new experiences as they arise.

In domestic dogs, this maturing process takes place under more artificial conditions. If a puppy is

Above: **A puppy gets his first taste of socialization playing (and competing) with his litter mates. This helps him learn give and take, and, as an adult, enables him better to cope with frustration.**

taken from its mother at the point of weaning (usually between seven and eight weeks) and brought into a household where he is the only dog in a 'pack' of humans, his key socialization stage, which occurs broadly between the ages of around eight and 16 weeks, needs to be very carefully managed.

It's at this age that puppies take in new experiences to saturation point, and imprint them into their subsequent behaviour. This extreme impressionability means that bad as well as good experiences have a disproportionately powerful effect, and may decide whether a puppy turns into a dog that expects the best from new people and happenings, or a more fearful dog, who approaches novel things with apprehension.

## FROM PUPPY TO ADULT PET

In the wild, experiences are accumulated naturally, within a larger group identity. For domestic dogs, socialization (except when managed by an exceptionally careful owner) can be a more hit-and-miss affair. Of course, not all the experiences of wild dogs will be positive. In fact, to take just a couple of examples, both the Asian dhole and the African wild dog have very high rates of both puppy and adult mortality. But the mere fact that a puppy is part of a community of his own kind will give him more developmental lessons and support than he's likely to get living with what is, after all, a different species.

You'll find notes on a practical socialization programme for puppies later in the book (see pages 86–7). The key is to constantly reinforce the behaviour you want to see, i.e. a calm, brave approach to unfamiliar objects, people or situations. A fearful puppy in the wild is unlikely to make a successful adult, and a fearful domestic dog can be a difficult pet.

If a puppy shows anxiety or fright, be sure to behave calmly and confidently yourself. Some training wisdom recommends that you simply ignore fearful behaviour. More recently, some behaviourists have suggested that the owner join the situation that's causing fear as calmly as possible and, if appropriate, redirect the puppy's attention to something positive, so that he doesn't build on his small fear, but is instead pleasantly distracted. This plays against natural human instinct – most people, confronted by a frightened puppy, would be inclined to pick it up and be comforting.

Whichever route you go, make sure that the puppy does not sense that *you* are frightened. Remaining calm and quiet should lead your puppy to conclude that there is nothing to fear.

## BASIC INSTINCT **Adult 'puppies'**

You can see remnants of puppyhood in the way a pet dog will sometimes act to appease its owner. Dogs who approach from the side to lick your face are exhibiting hardwired puppy behaviour – they may also try to lick the face of a 'senior' dog to show that, as juveniles, they don't pose a threat. Similarly, an anxious dog who is keen to avoid any power play will roll over on his back to reveal his belly. This is designed to stress how helpless he is.

# A sense of smell

How dogs experience the world around them is bound to affect how they behave. Dogs obviously do not perceive the world as we humans do – one of the biggest reasons being that they do not have the same capabilities of sight and smell.

Humans have a stronger sense of smell than we think (in experiments, blindfolded people could often smell the differences between familiar people and strangers without them speaking or the obvious prompts of characteristic perfumes, soaps and so on), but we rely on our sight and, to a lesser extent, our hearing for information about the world around us. Dogs are very different.

## 'SEEING' BY NOSE

Even the keenest-eyed sighthound – that is, a dog such as a greyhound or a saluki that has been selectively bred to hunt its prey by sight alone – has bad eyesight in human terms.

The ability of a sighthound to track visual movement is spectacular, but otherwise their vision is believed to be typically canine: they are colour-blind in the red/green spectrum and their world-view is greyish and blurred. Unless there is something in their sights that's moving in a way that might prompt a chase, sighthounds can't be said to have sharp sight.

Conversely, a dog's sense of smell is, compared with a person's, simply off the scale. It's an oft-quoted statistic that the scenting receptors of a dog are more than 44 times as strong as a human's. That's not to mention the flexibility and scent 'memory' that all dogs have inbuilt. It's believed that in a practical sense, a dog can smell something like two thousand times more powerfully than a person.

As you might well expect, the anatomy of a dog's nose is

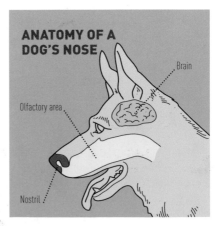

**ANATOMY OF A DOG'S NOSE**

Brain

Olfactory area

Nostril

## BASIC INSTINCT **Degrees of smell**

Dogs have varying degrees of scent-awareness. Scenthounds have the strongest sense of smell, and within this group the bloodhound is believed to have the most refined scenting mechanism. Other hunting and retrieving breeds have all scored high in comparative experiments. Even the least scent-aware dog, however, has a stronger and more sensitive sense of smell than a number of other species, not just humans.

complicated. Not only is the nose itself very flexible and mobile (it can move around more than the noses of most mammals without the dog having to turn its head), but it also boasts a shelf behind the nostrils that retains scent molecules when the dog sniffs. This storage system prevents smells being lost when the dog breathes out and enables him to retain and analyze scents.

Dogs also have a highly developed vomeronasal organ, which is an additional sensor formed of two sacs at the base of the septum. The vomeronasal organ is found in many other animals, but not often in such a developed state. It is mainly used to detect the presence of pheromones, the chemical messages that are carried between individuals of the same species. So not only can most dogs smell to a much more refined degree than people, they can also take in a lot of information about other dogs by reading their scent.

### SCENTS THAT DOGS LIKE

This part of dogs' sensory lives can account for actions we can't explain from a human point of view. While both dogs and people may enjoy the smell of a roasting chicken in the oven, the scents that we appreciate are strongly divergent elsewhere. Dogs dislike strongly perfumed scents or soaps (try offering a dog a wrist that you've just sprayed with your favourite product, and he'll probably turn away with a moue of distaste). Out walking, however, the same dog may be entranced by smells that disgust his owner, like fox faeces or dead duck. If the dog can find a way of transferring these smells to his coat, he'll do it.

Below: **Reading the news. Dogs can pick up an astonishing amount of information about other dogs simply by sniffing where they've been.**

# Canine body language

Over the last couple of decades there has been an increase in the amount of research carried out on communication between dogs. This has led to a higher awareness of the ways pet dogs communicate, both with each other and with humans.

Thanks to this, we can now move beyond speculation in deciding what dogs are feeling and, to a certain extent, interpret what they are trying to tell us. However, how much of their body language is instinctive and automatic, and which aspects of it are deliberately adopted to send messages to those around them is likely to remain a moot point.

The following pages offer a brief guide to the basics of canine body language. A close look at a dog's eyes, ears, mouth, face and tail, together with his general stance and demeanour, can tell you about what he is feeling.

## PUTTING IT ALL TOGETHER

In general, you have to learn to put signals together to read a dog with any accuracy. Some indicators will tell you about a dog's strength of feeling, but not necessarily what kind of feeling it is, while others will give you information about a dog's mood, but perhaps not how strongly he is feeling it. Put all these together, and a clear picture usually emerges.

It can't be said too strongly: dogs are extraordinarily skilled at sending out signs and most are equally good at reading them. You may find some surprises in what follows. If you thought a dog could only wag his tail in one way, you'll need to do some observation homework before you are able to pick up his nuances.

The physiognomy and shape of some breeds limits the freedom with which they can use their faces and bodies. Although they can be harder to read than other dogs, the signs are still there.

Right: **There's evidence that some body language is learned, not instinctive – so it's crucial to socialize a puppy carefully.**

# TIPS AND ADVICE
## What the tail tells us

The tail would seem a positive place to begin an overall tour of canine body language, as a wagging one is the sign universally recognized – by humans, at least – as an expression of joie de vivre. Look a little more carefully, though: not all tail movements equate to wagging. Here's a basic reading of common tail positions:

**TAIL MOVING FREELY BUT IN WIDE, SWEEPING ARCS, SLIGHTLY UP.** A classic wag. This is either a sign of happiness such as welcoming a visitor, for example, or of activity – a dog on the move – or both these states.

**TAIL CARRIED FREELY, NEITHER UP NOR DOWN, MOVING LOOSELY.** A tail in neutral. The dog isn't engaged with anything in particular, and is an observer in any activity going on around him.

**TAIL HELD RELATIVELY HIGH, MOVING FROM SIDE TO SIDE IN A SHORT ARC, SLIGHTLY STIFFLY.** This isn't a happy wag. Taken with other 'stay away' body signs, it should read as a warning. You might see it in a dog guarding something he values, or one which is feeling defensive.

**TAIL TUCKED WELL UNDER, BETWEEN THE BACK LEGS.** Usually a position taken up by a dog who's uncomfortable with his situation, or fearful about something. You might see this in a dog who is being fetched for a bath, or is unhappy about a visit to the veterinarian's.

**TAIL UP BUT HELD STILL.** A dog might take up this position just before launching into activity – you might see it in a dog which is assessing other dogs playing, for example, and deciding whether to join in.

## FACES

When reading a dog's face, it's best to take the mouth, eyes and ears separately and then consider the expression as a whole. The skill of 'reading' how a dog is feeling rests in your ability to add up the different signals and come up with the correct total. This is similar to the way in which you gauge how a person is feeling; you listen to their words and the tone in which these are spoken, but also look at the speaker's expression and stance.

## TONGUE FLICKS

Dogs often flick their tongues out over their noses or lips and back in again. It's a quick movement, but in some dogs you see it dozens of times a day. Behaviourists think that these tongue flicks are offered to other dogs as 'punctuation' – often acting as small warning or appeasement signals. For example, a dog about to pass another might flick his tongue because he is unsure of whether the other will tolerate him coming in to his body space.

## TIPS AND ADVICE
### What the eyes tell us

Because it's often hard to see a dog's pupil, and the whites of a dog's eyes usually show only in moments of high stimulation or when he's afraid, look at the muscles around the eye to get a feeling for what the expression is:

**RELAXED MUSCLES FORMING SMALL WRINKLES AROUND THE EYE.** The eye is not wide open but a little rounded A squinting expression combined with a rounded eye tends to indicate a relaxed and friendly dog. This is the eye you might expect to see at the opposite end of a broad, sweeping tail wag.

**EYES NARROWED AND FOCUSED WITH A 'HARD' LOOK.** These are signs of a dog under stress, giving rise to either aggression or fear. To establish which, try looking at the relative expression of the mouth.

**EYES WIDE OPEN, THE WHITES SHOWING, ROLLING SLIGHTLY.** The sclera, or white of the eye, tends to show when the dog is quite highly stimulated. It indicates strong feeling, but not necessarily what the feeling is – you would be just as likely to see it when the dog is enjoying a lively game as you would in the course of a scrap with another dog.

**TENSION IN OUTER CORNERS.** To read the expression on a dog's mouth, look at the corners as well as at the muzzle. The outer corners of a dog's mouth (the 'commissure') are pulled back or move forward when a dog feels pressured. Retracted corners indicate that the dog is feeling defensive, and may be fearful, while corners that are pushing forward indicate a state of mind that is potentially aggressive. Most of the time the commissure is in neutral: wrinkled neither forward nor back.

**OPEN MOUTH, TONGUE POSSIBLY PROTRUDING A LITTLE, NO TENSION IN MUZZLE.** This is the look on the face of a happy, relaxed dog. If two dogs are wrestling and you're not sure if it's friendly, look at their mouths. If they are open, with no tension wrinkles around the nose, the play is genuine.

**MOUTH VERY SLIGHTLY OPEN, WITH A SLIGHT 'BLOWN OUT' OR PUFFY LOOK AROUND THE LIPS, AND STILLNESS IN THE FACE.** This is a reactive expression; the dog is usually deciding how he feels about something going on around him, and is focusing his interest, which is slight rather than intense.

**MOUTH CLOSED, PUCKERING AND WRINKLING AROUND THE LIPS.** This is a 'growling' face. The dog may not actually be making any noise, but he's warning you off. Accompanied by a still or stiff tail, it's very much a request that you stay away.

**MOUTH CLOSED, FACE LOOSE, NO PUCKERING AROUND THE MUZZLE.** Usually indicates a focused look, when the dog is concentrating on something, but in neutral.

**MOUTH OPEN, CORNERS OF MOUTH PULLED BACK, MUZZLE WRINKLED, SOMETIMES TEETH SHOWING.**
An apprehensive or fearful expression. This is one to be treated with respect – as a dog that is afraid is a dog that may bite.

## EAR POSITIONS

Wild dogs have large, triangular, upright ears (in the case of the African wild dog, so extremely large that they give the animal a faintly comic look). These are the best ears for hearing with because they can turn towards noise and have a large, open channel down which the noise can travel. Ears like this are also easy for other pack members to see from far away, which means that any information can be spread quickly across relatively long distances.

In domestic dogs, there is such a wide range of ear shapes across the different breeds, from the long, exaggeratedly drooping flaps of the basset or the bloodhound to the upright, triangular shape of a German shepherd or an English bull terrier, that it can be hard in some cases to read their basic position.

If you're studying a dog that has one of the less obvious ear shapes, always look at the base of the ear – it's the point at which it's easiest to see where the ear is placed.

Even in the hardest-to-view breeds, you should be able to tell whether the ear is pointing forward or backward.

## BASIC INSTINCT Calming signs

The eminent Norwegian trainer and behaviourist Turid Rugaas has developed the theory, now widely accepted, that dogs send each other calming signals to keep their encounters and relationships good tempered and to deflect any potential conflict. Generally, even very small movements, particularly in a dog's face, can send big messages as to his mood.

The signals Rugaas refers to are relatively easy to spot and completely unambiguous. Watch out for the following behaviour when you see dogs interacting: one dog turning its head and body slightly sideways as another approaches; a dog suddenly turning its head down and sniffing the ground as it sees another dog, or sitting down and scratching. Rugaas argues that these are signs sent by well-socialized dogs that are universally recognized in the canine community, and have developed for the specific purpose of letting other animals know that a dog is peaceful.

If you watch a group of pet dogs who aren't familiar with one another interacting off-leash, it would be hard to disagree with Rugaas. You see the same movements used by different dogs again and again, and it's usually the dogs with the best and calmest canine manners who practise them most frequently.

# TIPS AND ADVICE
## What the ears tell us

Ears are generally less revealing than the eyes or mouth, but reading their position can add considerably to the overall picture of a dog's mood, by showing you how stimulated he is, for example:

**EAR UPRIGHT AND FACING FORWARD (IN OPEN, TRIANGULAR EAR SHAPES), AND PLACED SLIGHTLY FORWARD ON THE HEAD.** This is best described as a ready-for-action ear. The dog is alert and ready to react. It does not, however, tell you anything about the nature of the stimulus.

**EAR PULLED SLIGHTLY BACK AND CLOSE TO THE HEAD.** An indication that the dog is slightly nervous or apprehensive about what he sees or hears.

**EARS STRONGLY FORWARD AND UPRIGHT.** This ear position indicates a strong degree of arousal, without an apprehensive element. It is a forceful sign of confidence, meaning that the dog is interested in something and is ready to act on it. Depending on circumstances, and the rest of the dog's body language, it could be a pointer that the dog is on the offensive and may be aggressive. If the ears are flattened slightly and out to the side (not the back), it is even more likely that the dog is on the offensive.

**EARS PULLED HARD BACKWARDS, TIGHT TO THE HEAD.** Usually a sign that the dog is both defensive and fearful. If the ears are also pointing slightly downwards, it's a sign that fear is uppermost. These are the ears you might see on a dog that is trying to back away from a situation rather than coming forward to deal with it.

## WHOLE-BODY LANGUAGE

We've looked at how to read the body language at either end of a dog – his tail and head. But what about the parts in between: his body and overall stance? The mood of some dogs is so obvious to the onlooker it doesn't require conscious reading – the dog happily running around playing, for example, or the reluctant dog being dragged to the veterinarian. These kind of automatic observations are down in large part to the dog's stance: his legs and the line of his back (top line).

A relaxed dog will have an easy, tension-free top line. Stress will cause the back to round slightly, and a fearful or worried animal will have a definite convex curve to his top line. A rounded back combined with a tucked tail is a clear sign that

Above: Has the dog in the front found a particularly fascinating smell, or is he taking time out from the others, sending a signal that says 'I'm not involved'?

the dog is apprehensive. Add braced legs to the mix and you're looking at a tense or unhappy dog. Similarly, a very straight top line, with no movement at all, contributes to the characteristic 'frozen' look of a tense dog, deciding what action to take.

The way a dog holds its legs can tell you whether it wants to move forwards. A dog that is uncertain may appear to be approaching a situation, but his back legs will be braced, pulling his body slightly back. A confident dog moves forward with its whole body, including its legs. A nervous dog will be more ambivalent and send mixed messages with its body language.

## ADDING THINGS UP

To discover your dog's state of mind, read his whole body: look at each body part in turn, interpret the signs and then add them up. This way you're most likely to get an accurate overall picture.

You should always study the context in which you're watching a dog too. If a dog has a slightly raised, still tail, a relaxed, open mouth, ears turned slightly forward and focused but rounded eyes, for example, look at what is holding his attention.

If he's looking out of the window down the street, he may have just caught sight of his owner's car parking up and be excited at the thought of seeing her. If he's outdoors and watching a group of dogs playing together, the likeliest reading is that he's weighing things up before joining in.

## TALKING DOGS

Dogs don't only talk with their bodies – they have voices too. However, compared with humans – incessant talkers by canine standards – dogs vocalize only rarely. How much of the noise they make is an involuntary expression of how they are feeling, and how much consists of deliberate signals is a moot point.

However, research carried out into different pitches and levels of barking seems to indicate that barks can be used to signal different messages, from a basic 'I am here' to a 'Want to play?' invitation. Often, with practice, it's actually easier to read a dog by looking at his body language than by listening to him.

Below: **Aggression or a warning signal? This dog is showing plenty of teeth, but the muscles around his eyes and the corners of his mouth are quite relaxed.**

# Dominance and submission

The idea of dominant and submissive dogs was once a widely accepted concept and a key part of dog behaviour studies and dog training, and it still lies at the heart of many of the older training regimes and manuals.

Over the past few years, however, doubt has been cast on how accurate a reading of dog behaviour and character it offers. To many dog behaviourists the word 'dominant' has become discredited to the extent that it is no longer used to describe any aspects of dog character or dog behaviour.

Unfortunately, the idea of the dominant dog, which must be made to submit to its owner (often by force), is still quite widely in circulation. Most pet owners will encounter it at some time or other, whether in a book, as hearsay from other dog owners, or from a trainer or behaviourist who is using outdated methods. In order to understand why the dominance/submission training and ideas are falling out of favour, it's worth spending some time looking at the theory that underlies them. Most dog lovers believe that the newer training methods are gentler, more humane and, crucially, more effective.

Left: It's hard to tell whether this dog is showing 'submission' to her owner or whether the owner has actually been 'trained' to deliver a belly rub whenever her pet rolls over – the latter looks the more likely.

## SUBMISSION

For many years it was thought that pet dogs were essentially wolves living in human homes, which had to be taught – often forcefully – to live by human rules. Wolves live in packs, and those members of the pack who have lower status show deference to wolves with higher status by rolling on their backs and showing their bellies in a display of submission.

You often see dogs assuming this position naturally – puppies will frequently roll on their backs in front of an adult, particularly if they're feeling under pressure, and adult dogs will bow and roll submissively before a dog that they find somewhat intimidating. In fact, some very timid dogs will do this almost every time that another dog approaches them.

## TRAINING METHODS

Gradually, a training theory developed around the idea that if an owner could force a dog into a position of submission, the dog would recognize the owner as a leader and would automatically respect and defer to him. Out of this theory came a number of exercises that revolved around showing the dog who was boss. They included taking a puppy and shaking it hard by the scruff of the neck when it misbehaved, regardless of what the 'misbehaviour' was (from urinating in the house to fighting with another dog) and a move called the 'dominance rollover', or the 'alpha rollover', which involved the dog being picked up and thrown down on its back while the owner stood over it.

Above: **Eye whites showing, tense muzzle, closed mouth and lowered head all indicate a dog who is very tense, but in a defensive rather than an offensive way.**

Unsurprisingly, more enlightened behaviourists soon began to criticize these methods as causing far more problems than they solved. Often the dog didn't understand what he had done to deserve such forceful correction. In high-status dogs that were not easily made fearful, the result was sometimes aggression towards the owner. Also, more apprehensive types could be reduced to cowering, being constantly fearful of correction without understanding how it could be avoided.

Over time, it became clear that even wolves don't use these kinds of tactics to reinforce their status with one another. On the contrary, they tend to be naturally tolerant with their puppies and to avoid forceful corrections. The focus on dominance was deemed unworkable by many, and as a result, alpha rollovers and other such moves are becoming rarer.

## STATUS AT HOME

What the fans of the old dominance theories didn't take into account is how intelligent dogs are, and how much they are concerned with their own wellbeing. Provided that a dog knows, and is clear about, which behaviour results in good things – such as attention, food treats and games – the average dog, unless he has acquired a lot of behavioural baggage previously, will go for the behaviour that pays off.

A dog that is confident of being treated fairly and that knows what to expect isn't any more likely to behave in a 'dominant' way than one that's been bullied into submission.

There appears to be a wide range of status-awareness in dogs, just as there is amongst humans and any other animals that live in social groups. The internal arrangements of most of these groups, of whatever species, tend to revolve around the apportioning of the resources available, with the higher-status individuals getting to make most of the decisions regarding which member gets what.

We have no means of knowing whether dogs are aware that humans are a different species, but they certainly know that in a human household, people have control of most of the resources (attention, food, toys) that they value. Whether or not they happily accept that control or challenge it has to do with their perception of their own position in the status quo.

Provided that they get the food, attention and exercise that they want and that their owners want to give them, many dogs don't appear to think about status at all, accepting more or less whatever standing in the household that they are given.

Below: **Dogs will not usually behave in a 'dominant' way as long as they are given enough attention, food, treats and games.**

Right: **A dog who isn't very status-conscious may be content to let both other dogs and people around him call the shots.**

Conversely, most people will have encountered clever and strong-minded dogs who will push the boundaries of what's allowed at home and who have worked out ways of getting what they want without direct conflict with their owners.

Dogs have to live in a human world, so even though the idea of 'master' has largely given way to 'leader' in the vocabulary of trainers, it is important that your dog does see you as a leader as well as a companion. What has changed completely from the bad old days of domination theory is the view of how it's best for an owner to lead.

Careful, logical and consistent behaviour around dogs tends to result in pets who can work out that, based on their experience,

cooperation with humans pays. A dog that is benefiting from the relationship may see little reason to challenge it.

## RULES TO LIVE BY

Whether or not a dog cares about his relative place in the hierarchy, the best way to maintain good dog–human relations is to learn how to communicate with him in ways that he understands. Animal society of every kind has its own rules of behaviour and good manners, and dogs are just as able to accept rules as humans are.

To explain the rules to the dogs, though, we need to learn to talk to dogs just as fluently as they can talk to us. The next pages look at ways in which we can learn to do this.

# Talking to dogs

Dogs don't talk much – not with sound, anyway – but humans talk incessantly. Most pets seem to accept it good humouredly as just what humans do, but what they must think of the constant chatter can only be guessed at.

Because our own behaviour comes naturally to us, and because humans have a tendency to regard themselves as the top species, it can be difficult to accept the idea that what seems ordinary, everyday social behaviour to people is no more a universal norm than canine behaviour is.

Humans are as much at the mercy of species-specific hardwiring when it comes to behaviour as dogs are – and dogs, of course, have their own particular set of canine instincts. It's where the different species meet, each conforming to what's normal for them, that sometimes behavioural misunderstandings can arise and cause problems.

Below: **The eye contact and the arm wrapped around his neck are acceptable to this terrier from someone familiar to him – but it's strictly human behaviour.**

## TIPS AND ADVICE
### Do what I do not what I say

Most dog owners or enthusiasts recognize the range of behaviours that it's hard for dogs to learn. But something that's hard for a dog to learn could equally be looked on as something that's hard for a human to teach. Here are a few examples:

People find it incredibly difficult not to repeat commands. To teach a dog to respond to 'sit', you need to say 'sit'. But some dogs (probably the majority of dogs) first learned to sit in response to 'sit, sit, SIT, SIT, SIT!' That's because humans in general find it extraordinarily hard to stop talking and to respond to something – like a puppy's failure to get the concept of 'sit' first time – with an intelligent silence. It's almost comical how tough it is for someone to keep quiet having given the command, even after a trainer has told them to and they're consciously trying. It goes against our instincts, and once you appreciate how hard that is, it becomes much easier to respect for our dogs' willingness – and ability – to work against theirs.

Equally difficult, it seems, is for a human to ask a dog to do something using the same words every time. Since dogs don't use words – words are far too abstract a concept to appeal to a dog for their own sake – they need to use quite a sophisticated sequence of thoughts to connect specific words with specific instructions. What can we expect them to make of an instruction to 'sit' when it is embedded in a string of words such as, 'Sit, good boy, Jem, no I said down! Sit....'? This is even worse than repeating the same command umpteen times. It's almost impossible for a dog to pick out the relevant parts of the instruction, and certainly impossible to know what to make of the rest. Our urge to talk is so strong that it overcomes our knowledge that this isn't the best way to make ourselves clear – not to a dog, in any case.

Another mix that's difficult for a dog to interpret is a verbal instruction combined with human body language that appears to contradict it. Perhaps the most typical example of this is the request to a dog to 'come!' combined with a step or two in his direction. Dogs understand it if you move in the direction in which you want them to move, in the same way that they will look in the direction in which you are looking. Moving towards them while asking them to move towards you is, in canine terms, a straight contradiction. From a dog's point of view, to walk away from him and ask him to 'come' is a more logical sequence, and one that he can understand.

Above: **Restrained by their leads, these two dogs are meeting face to face. Natural to people, in dog terms this probably feels uncomfortably direct.**

It's not only the talk that comes out of our mouths that can be confusing, but also our body talk, which can send out similarly misleading messages to our pets. Again, the problems are caused simply by each species doing what comes naturally: humans behaving like primates and dogs reacting like canines. Dogs are disconcertingly observant of human body language, too, so they respond to the messages that they think they are seeing – whether the person 'sending' them is aware of it or not.

## PRAISE AND ATTENTION

Almost all dogs love to have human attention. The rare exceptions are very shy dogs or dogs that have been abused and have learned to associate attention with bad, rather than good things. So it's worth learning how to greet an unfamiliar dog – or how to pet a familiar one – in ways he'll like. The body language of primates and canines is radically different, even when it comes to a simple 'hello'. Humans love a straightforward approach: direct, if brief, eye contact, and perhaps a warm hug. And while one might hesitate a little before greeting, say, an orangutan in the same way; if you did, it's likely that the orangutan would at least recognize you as a fellow primate.

## WHAT DOGS WANT

Dogs see things very differently. Every element of a primate–primate greeting must look unnatural, bordering on discourteous to a dog. At the fundamental level, taking a direct approach, head-on, primate-style, isn't deemed friendly from a dog's point of view. Friendly dogs approach one another from sideways on. Often they start from the rear, picking up information by nose before moving on to a face-to-face greeting. Looking another dog in the eye may be read as confrontational between dogs. More normally, one dog will glance towards the other and then away again (the 'hard-eye' stare that a dog will use when he wants to be confrontational is very easily recognizable; it isn't a friendly look).

In canine terms, a hug could be read as threatening. Though a popular move between primates, from humans to orangutans, it seems like a status-seeking attempt to a dog. If you hug your dog, you need to lay a 'paw' on his shoulder, which places you on a higher level than him. To a dog, this doesn't add up to a greeting between equals.

That said, you may be used to patting or hugging your own dog, and your dog may seem to graciously accept your attention. It's doubtful whether he's really enjoying it. Many pets have learned to be tolerant of human body language, but there are few who, if offered the choice, would opt for a human hug over a belly rub.

## CHECKLIST
### Good ways to meet and greet

It's usually dogs that have to adjust to the human way of doing things. Sometimes it's a good idea to switch it round and try to see things from a dog's point of view such as:

- **STAND WELL BACK.** You are almost certainly taller than the dog you are greeting, and he won't appreciate you towering over him, any more than you would like another person looming over you and invading your personal space.
- **IF THE DOG YOU'RE APPROACHING DOESN'T COME FORWARD** to greet you, don't approach him. Stay still and look away, focusing on something else in the room, and turning your head slightly. This sends a calming signal to a nervous dog, giving him time to collect himself and decide whether to make an approach.

- **HOLD YOUR HAND OUT** a little if the dog approaches you, but make sure it's within the dog's view. Contrary to popular (human) belief, most dogs dislike being patted on top of the head. It means that they can't see where your hand is, and, while many dogs enjoy stroking, they don't like a staccato 'patting' rhythm on their heads. Most dogs, once they've approached and sniffed you, will appreciate a gentle scratch or rub either under the chin or around the side of the face or the ears.

# Dogs and play

Humans play all their lives, and so do domestic dogs. We are unusual in this – adults in most other species stop playing as they mature. A love of play is something we have in common with dogs, and it helps form strong bonds between us.

## DOGS PLAYING TOGETHER

One piece of canine body language that's almost as widely seen as a wagging tail, is the play bow: the movement in which a dog goes down on his forepaws, rear in the air, with the obvious intention of initiating a game. It seems to be universally acknowledged between dogs, and is used not only at the beginning of games but at breaks in play, to signal the point at which the chasing dog becomes the one who is chased, or else that the dog who has the toy is ready for his playmate to make a bid to grab it.

That dogs enjoy play for its own sake is confirmed by the fact that unevenly matched dogs will often even up their abilities to prolong a game. A stronger dog may 'allow' a smaller or weaker animal to have a coveted toy for a bit just to have the joy of chasing it, while a faster dog may slow down to allow a slower one to catch him. At the end of a play session the natural order and social ranking between dogs will assert itself, but during the game a tacit agreement is made that the play itself is the point of the exercise.

Left: **A classic play bow, frequently seen in every type of dog, whatever the breed, and whichever his preferred sort of play.**

## PLAYING WITH PETS

Although dogs can be very dog-focused when it comes to play, most are happy to extend their repertoire and to play with humans too. Dogs who have grown up primarily with people and without much canine company may even come to prefer playing with people.

Learning a few play signals that dogs recognize may increase your readability as a play companion – picking exactly the right time to pause at the key moments in the course of a game, for example, can heighten the level of anticipation and excitement for your dog.

Vary both the games you play and the toys you play with to ensure that play doesn't become boring for either of you. For game ideas that will build on the bond you already have with your dog and encourage enthusiastic obedience, see chapter four.

Although dogs may become less playful as they get older, regular games are good for them and are a way of making sure that you spend quality time together, rather than simply living side by side without interacting. An interest in playing can also keep an older dog young in spirit, and maintain his fitness levels.

Play workouts can be used to exercise a dog's brain as well as his body, so it's well worth experimenting with a wide range of games and toys however old a pet is, or whatever his breed – he may even surprise you with unexpected skills or talents.

This chapter is concerned with behaviour rather than behavioural problems, but before moving on to how to choose a dog that's right for you, it's worth stressing the underlying need of all dogs, which is to feel safe, and that they know their role.

It's not known to what extent dogs are analytical thinkers, or whether they can distinguish between species – that is, whether they understand that humans are not dogs and vice versa. What is known is that dogs do not rationalize to the extent that humans can, and that, for a dog to be happy and content, he must know where he belongs in the pattern around him. A dog that is both highly social and status-conscious may be completely lost without some degree of guidance as to his place in the 'pack', even if the rest of the pack is human rather than canine.

Above: **Uncertain of his surroundings, this dog has taken shelter with his human leader, confident that she can provide the most effective protection.**

## A WORKING ROLE

When most domestic dogs were working animals and dogs that were purely kept as pets were rare, the focus of a dog would be the job that he had to do, whether it was as a hunter, a herder, or a draught animal that pulled loads.

Today, when so many are kept as companions, the jobs available to most dogs are limited. However, dogs need to be kept occupied mentally as well as exercised physically, and a bright, bored dog can develop behavioural problems.

It's important to ensure that a pet dog not only knows his place in the social structure around him, but that he is also given enough to do within that role.

## WHO'S IN CHARGE?

Unless a pet dog is aware of who is leading his 'group', he may take a unilateral decision to assume the leadership role. Behaviourists agree that this can lead to all kinds of problems. If a dog starts to believe he is leader of the household, he might for example, feel the need to herd 'his' children around the house and (worse) nip them for perceived misbehaviours, as he would any puppies in his charge. Equally, he might suffer from separation anxiety, if his owners have gone out and his instinct tells him that he should be in charge of the situation – how can he look after his 'people' when he doesn't know where they are?

It isn't a problem you might immediately identify as status-related, but it could be, depending on the dog. A dog may not need a master in the old-fashioned sense, but if he lives in a human household he'll be happier if he's led rather than being put in a position where he feels he must try to lead.

Above: **In the wild, status carries big responsibilities. A dog who feels he should be in control of his domestic surroundings, however, may make a difficult pet.**

## STATUS AT HOME

On page 31 we discussed what decides dog to dog status in the natural world. A clear indicator of his ranking is an individual's ability to get what he wants, regardless of the means of getting it. Status tends to crop up at home when a dog wants something he isn't getting: a toy that another dog is playing with, perhaps. It's how he tries to get it that tells you how secure he is. A confident dog will simply take what he wants. A dog who sees himself as lower in the ranking but who aspires to higher things will try to get the toy, but less confidently. And the dog that is happy with low status will indicate what he wants but give up if it's not easily granted to him. All three live in a world run by human rules, so even the high-status dog needs to know that the resources are controlled by you and are within your gift.

# Choosing a dog

Once you've decided that you want a dog, you need to decide what type. Pedigree or mutt, large or small, canine exercise junkie or couch potato? Would you like a puppy from a professional breeder or an older dog from a shelter? You need to be sure that the dog you fall in love with is one that you'll be able to stick with for the rest of his life, so advance homework is important. Take the time to read the following pages thoroughly and you won't be faced with the heartache of a pet that's poorly matched with the home you can provide. Checklists and questionnaires enable you to assess your suitability as an owner and guide you towards the dog whose running costs, exercise needs and natural temperament will suit you best.

As well as examining the pros and cons of buying from a breeder, this chapter gives you tips on how to find your dream dog at a shelter. The intention, above all, is to increase your awareness of what to expect from your new dog before he arrives, to give your long-term relationship the best chance of success.

# Why do you want a dog?

Before you pick up a breed guide or visit a dog shelter and look at the dogs they have, think hard about why it is that you want a dog. There are plenty of great reasons for wanting to add a canine member to your household and a few that aren't so good.

The more honest you are with yourself about why you'd like a dog, the easier it will be to pick out the right pet from the host of options available. Consider whether you want an exercise buddy, a family pet or an amusing companion who won't be too demanding and won't answer back. How much time can you commit?

And, realistically, you must consider what you can afford to spend, not just on acquiring a dog, but on the day-to-day costs.

Below: **Puppies grow up. Don't buy a dog 'for the children' if you don't want one yourself.**

## THINK IT THROUGH

Often, potential owners don't properly analyze why it is that they want a dog. In some cases, if they asked themselves some tough questions, they might think again. Dogs are famously tolerant and loving companions, good exercise buddies and playful friends, but they're a long-term responsibility, with lives and opinions of their own to be taken into account. They can't simply be taken back to the shop if things don't work out.

Have a careful look at the list of not-so-good reasons for wanting a dog. They are common enough motivations, but are unlikely to lead to a happy situation. Generally

## Check your motivation

Don't start by asking 'which dog?'. The first real question is 'dog or no dog?'.
What are your real reasons for wanting one?

### Good reasons for wanting a dog...

🐾 You want to get fitter and think that a dog would be a great incentive to exercise.

🐾 You've always loved dogs and have moved into a house with more space and a big garden – it's the first time you've really lived somewhere suitable for a pet.

🐾 You've just retired, you're living on your own and you have plenty of time for a dog.

🐾 The family is growing up and you think that both you and your older kids would enjoy playing with and exercising a dog.

### ... and some not-so-good ones

🐾 The kids have been nagging you for a dog for ages. If you give in, they'll probably do most of the hard work.

🐾 You've always wanted a (insert breed of your choice here); you just love how they look.

🐾 You're out at work all day and you want some undemanding companionship in the evenings.

🐾 A friend has just bought an adorable puppy and you want one just like it.

🐾 You've recently begun working from home and think a dog will provide company during the day.

speaking, younger children don't make great dog carers once the novelty of the new pet has worn off.

Be wary of taking on a breed simply because you like the look of it. If you don't do plenty of homework, you could have some surprises as you discover its less well-publicized characteristics. Working outside the home all day and then expecting your dog to sit calmly with you when you finally get in is unrealistic. Your friend's adorable puppy? It won't necessarily translate well when you are responsible for your own version. It's obvious when you think about it.

## GOOD REASONS

On the other hand, good reasons for wanting a dog abound. Dogs are great company for reasonably active people who live alone; many dogs are good exercise-persuaders – pleading canine eyes can have the power to coax even a couch potato up and out for a walk; and someone who's previously lived in cramped accommodation may legitimately see a move to a house with a garden as a milestone to be celebrated by getting a dog. So don't let yourself be put off – just be realistic about your circumstances before going out to find your pet.

# What dogs need

All dogs, regardless of what breed or size they are, need food and water, training, comfortable shelter, health care and exercise. As dogs are social animals, they also need company. Regular play is important too.

## FEEDING

Dogs' feeding needs vary as much as their size, so the cost of feeding them will vary, too. Assess the diet of a dog and the quantities in which he eats with the breeder or the shelter before you commit. A tiny dog may not need a huge amount of food, but may need a particular type of diet. A large dog may eat a lot but thrive on quite basic fare. And, of course, there's always the possibility that you acquire a large dog with specific dietary needs, so that your pet's diet not only needs careful consideration

Below: **When you're assessing what your future pet might eat, look at the quality as well as the quantity.**

but also needs to be supplied in substantial quantities! There are healthy and economical ways of feeding every dog – even the most delicate digestion doesn't need to be pampered with steak – but it's good to know whether you're taking on a chow-it-all-down type or a fussy eater. You'll find information on a whole range of feeding options in chapter three (see pages 98–101).

## TRAINING

Even if you're not planning to enter your pet for Canine Citizen of the Year, you'll need to dedicate plenty of time to training – and, if you're getting a puppy, that includes house training over the first few months, too. Training is necessary for every dog, puppy or adult, large or small, and can be quite time-consuming.

Think in terms of daily short sessions for the first 18 months if you're getting a puppy, and probably longer if you have one of the slower-maturing breeds.

If you're looking for an adult dog, most of those available will have had some training but are likely to need at least a refresher course in a new home. Obedience and training classes help, but act as reinforcement for the training work you're putting in at home; they won't do the job for you.

House training can take a long or a short time, depending on breed and individual dog, but it will almost always take a few months before you cease to have 'accidents' indoors. Young dogs, too, aren't able to wait as long as mature ones, so make sure a new puppy is given the opportunity to go outside every hour or so to start with.

## GROOMING

If you choose a sleek, short-coated dog, bathing and grooming won't be much of an issue. If you are drawn to lavish long coats, however, you'll find that they don't stay that way unless your dog has regular baths and time spent on him with a brush and comb.

Dogs can't groom themselves, but tangles and knots are uncomfortable, so they may try if you don't do it for them or get a professional to help. Check out the advice on coat care whichever type of dog you're considering. Some dogs are heavy shedders – either year-round or in seasonal moults – whereas others hardly moult at all. It's important to know what to expect in advance.

Above: **Long, thick coats can call for a lot of time-consuming care particularly If your dog is an energetic type, keen on playing in water and mud.**

## SHELTER

As well as the specific space your dog will sleep in, 'shelter' is a blanket term for the space a dog is going to take up in your house. Almost all companion dogs live indoors; how much dedicated or shared space you want your dog to have is up to you.

Think ahead – a large, exuberant dog, equipped with a basket and possibly a crate, too, may take up more of your living quarters than you envisaged. You'll decide whether your dog is allowed on the furniture, to go upstairs and so on, but most dogs need a certain amount of one-to-one time, particularly if they live in a single-dog household.

## HEALTH CARE

Your dog will need a veterinarian, both for regular check-ups and for any health problems or emergencies. This is one of the less predictable aspects of owning a pet, as health needs vary hugely. Much like people, some dogs will hardly see a veterinarian from one year to the next, while others may seem to need appointments almost weekly.

While you can research your chosen breed of dog carefully and do your homework about any potential health issues, it's never possible to predict with complete accuracy how much professional care a dog will need.

## EXERCISE

All dogs need exercise, but how much and what kind depends enormously on the type and breed. Size isn't always a guide – although the very tiniest dogs tend not to need a huge amount of walking, even if they're quite energetic, purely because they're so small. Greyhounds need the chance to run, but tire quite quickly and are famously calm and quiet at home, while young, energetic spaniels, retrievers and collies are almost impossible to wear out. Some small but feisty breeds – a definition into which a lot of terriers fall – need more exercise than their compact size would suggest.

How you manage it will depend on your lifestyle, but most dogs will need one long or two moderate walks per day, plus a couple of brief constitutionals. Bear in mind that dogs naturally have the most energy at the beginning and the end of the day (the technical term for this is 'crepuscular'), so evening and morning walks tie in best with their internal timetables, while often suiting a human schedule too.

## PLAY

Play may not be a 'need' in the same sense as food and exercise but, given the chance, most dogs love to play in one way or another; whether it's with other dogs, chasing a ball thrown by their owner, retrieving a toy or playing tug. When you're planning your dog's regular exercise schedule, factor in playtime.

Play builds bonds with your dog, can give him a 'job' to do (often valuable for traditional working breeds who need mental stimulation as well as straightforward exercise) and varies his walks and face-to-face time with you in a healthy and enjoyable way. Play can be as beneficial for the owner as it is for the dog – watching your dog have fun is a proven relaxant and de-stresser.

## UNDERSTANDING

Although it's last on the list, understanding dogs – your dog, in particular – is a modern addition to the pet-owner's requirement list. Twenty or 30 years ago owners wouldn't have thought that they needed to get inside a dog's head in order to keep him, but with an increase in the amount of research into pet behaviour it's become possible for people to 'read' their pet dogs quite accurately.

This knowledge can both strengthen owners' relationships with their pets and avoid behavioural problems that arise from species-to-species misunderstandings rather than inherent character defects. Understanding your dog calls for you to take the time to observe him and to read up a little on dog behaviour. It's well worth the effort, and it costs nothing.

Below: **Lively play sessions with other dogs ensure your pet gets plenty of socialization practice – and tires him out too.**

# What dogs cost

Dogs don't necessarily need to cost a lot, but any animal that lives with you permanently comes with running costs. To make sure that you can afford a dog, it's a good idea to draw up an annual cost projection for the dog you have in mind.

Before you commit to a particular breed/size/type, ask the breeder, the veterinarian or the pet shop about the likely costs. Include both the one-off expenses and running costs. Some of your numbers will be guesswork, but even an informed guess will give you a ballpark figure, and will help you avoid any financial surprises when you get your pet.

## VETERINARY BILLS

Visits to the veterinarian are by far the highest cost most dogs incur in the course of their lives. You can choose a dog with as few inherent health risks as possible, but the safest way to cover the costs is to take out pet insurance (see page 157).

Although a full policy can be quite expensive, the monthly or annual payments can be factored into your budget in advance, making them easier to manage than a large, unexpected bill, should your dog fall seriously ill or have an accident.

Veterinarian fees can become very high, running easily into thousands if your dog needs a complicated operation. Research the best pet insurance deals online and in veterinarian surgeries, magazines etc. – there are plenty of offers and deals available. Ask other pet owners, as they will often have had direct experience of different policies.

Left: **A sick dog can be a very, very expensive dog – especially if he needs an operation or long-term courses of drug treatment.**

# CHECKLIST
## Budgeting for a dog

Working out a budget helps you to think around all the implications of owning a dog – not just the financial aspect, but also the changes in schedule and the investment in time that will be involved. Make a list to check you have included everything:

## One-time costs

**COLLAR/LEASH**
x 3 if you are working out costs for a puppy, because you'll need at least three different sizes as he grows.

**BED AND/OR CRATE**
For a puppy, budget for an adjustable crate with internal partitions. These can be removed so you don't have to buy a new crate for your dog when he reaches his full adult size.

**BOWLS**
For food and water.

**GROOMING TOOLS**
Brush and nail clippers.

**TOYS**
Rubber ball, tug toy, treats.

**TOTAL:**

## Running costs

**FOOD**
Find out how much an adult dog of the same size/species eats, and multiply across a year.

**VETERINARIAN COSTS**
Factor in vaccinations, insurance and worming/de-fleaing treatments.

**HOLIDAY COSTS**
This will depend on your situation but is likely to include the cost of a pet-sitter or kennels.

**GROOMING**
Allow for at least two sessions at a groomer's per year if you're getting a breed that needs professional bathing/grooming/clipping.

**YEARLY TOTAL:**

**OVERALL COST FOR FIRST YEAR:**

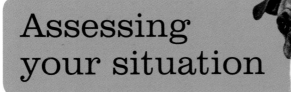

# Assessing your situation

You've looked at what dogs need, and worked out what a pet will cost. Now it's time for a look at your own lifestyle and how you envisage a dog will fit in. There is a dog to suit almost everyone, but it's important to be realistic about what you can offer.

Someone with a full-time job and a busy life may not be the best owner for a bouncy, young golden retriever. That doesn't mean that you can't make your ideal dog fit with your life, provided that you're prepared to compromise if it proves necessary.

## DOGS AND CHILDREN

Many of us remember the dogs of our childhood with great affection, and having a family pet can be a good experience all round: for adults,

children and dog. But someone in the family still needs to be that dog's primary carer, and that carer won't be a child, however hard they beg for a pet and promise to do everything from walking to grooming and feeding. They won't pay for it, either, so if you don't really want a dog yourself and don't have the time or the money to care for one properly, don't get one for the children's sake.

Similarly, while dogs can be marvellous companions for older children who have respect for them, many dogs can find toddlers and younger children frightening and unpredictable. Children do a lot of things that upset dogs, from high-pitched screaming to squeezing, pinching and hugging unexpectedly. Even a mellow dog can find their behaviour alarming, and a nervous or easily aroused dog become snappy, fearful and ultimately aggressive. For these reasons it's crucial that contact between children and dogs

Left: **Children need to be carefully taught how to behave sensibly and calmly around dogs.**

is always supervised by an adult. The children as well as the dog should be carefully trained in their behaviour towards one another.

When you're choosing a family dog, too, don't let your heart rule your head. Listen to what breeders and other owners tell you about a specific breed. If it sounds inappropriate for your circumstances, or if you're not experienced with dogs and the breed you favour will call for a lot of dedicated training and exercise time, aim for something a little less demanding that you'll be able more easily to incorporate into your life.

Dog shelters are full of young adult dogs that were acquired as puppies but became too demanding to fit around the requirements of a young family as they grow up. Don't make the same mistake. It may be easier to get an adult dog in the first place, so that you can start as you mean to go on, rather than trying to adjust as your cute puppy grows into a demanding canine teenager.

## DOGS AND HOLIDAYS

Think, too, about who's going to look after your pet when you are away from home. Dogs need companionship as well as food and exercise while you're gone. Are you going to use kennelling, an in-house pet-sitter, or rely on friends? Do you go on the sort of trips (beach holidays, country breaks, camping) that allow for pets, or do you prefer the sort of breaks that rule out canine companionship? There are plenty of options when it comes to

Above: **Local holidays that you can enjoy with your dog can be just as much fun for you as they are for him.**

choosing dog care while you're away, but the best of them require booking in advance and careful planning.

## LOCAL SPACE

Take your everyday circumstances, into consideration. Where is your dog going to take his walks? Do you have a local park, or do you have to drive a distance to get to somewhere where he can run around off-leash? When are you going to fit walks in? Will your dog spend most of his time with you, or will he have to spend large chunks of his day home alone?

Dogs are extremely adaptable and, provided their needs are met, they can be happy in a flat or a large house in the city, the suburbs or the country. It's only fair to consider whether you've got the circumstances to give a dog a pleasant life rather than just a bearable one.

# Breed vs mutt

If your heart isn't set on a particular pedigree, consider the advantages of a cross-breed. 'Cross-breed' is the polite term for a mongrel or mutt: a direct cross between two pure-bred dogs or something much less traceable.

Owners of particularly unusual 'Heinz 57' dogs, for example, can entertain themselves for hours guessing which breed in their pet's remote ancestry is responsible for its distinctive ears or paws.

At the planned end of the market, a successful cross can create an entirely new model, which acquires a high demand and may eventually be recognized as a breed in itself.

The labradoodle (a mix of Labrador and poodle) is an example of this. At the more accidental end of the market, cross-breeds are simply a result of unplanned breeding.

## ADVANTAGES OF MONGRELS

Mongrel aficionados are quick to point out the advantages of cross-bred dogs. The strongest argument is that mongrels don't have the genetic health issues and problems of many pure-breeds. Some pedigree dogs come from a relatively small breeding group and thus a small gene pool, and have been bred for generations to strengthen certain aspects of their appearance – the flat face of the English bulldog, for example, didn't occur by breeding chance.

However, other genetic glitches are often unavoidably bred in along the way, leading to a predisposition to particular illnesses and conditions in many

Left: **An impressive pedigree from top-grade working stock won't always signify the perfect family pet.**

popular breeds. While responsible breeders will always do their very best to breed away from these predispositions there's no guarantee that they'll succeed. Mongrels – with an unlimited gene pool to call their own – often have stronger constitutions.

The same can be true of temperament. Character faults can be an unwelcome side-effect of over-breeding although, just as with health problems, a good breeder will do their best to overcome them. This doesn't of course mean that you're guaranteed a rock-solid character and an absence of health concerns if you choose a mongrel. But you are likely to have improved the odds.

Right. **Mongrels come in all shapes and sizes; few owners can resist trying to work out exactly which breeds made a contribution to their pet's ancestry.**

## WHERE TO FIND YOUR MUTT

First port of call for most mongrel-fanciers should be the local dog shelter (see pages 64–7), where you're likely to find plenty of choice. They may even be able to offer puppies. Mongrels are also often found through friends or family contacts. The disadvantage of a mongrel puppy of unknown parentage is that you cannot be sure how big he will grow, or what his characteristics may be. If you dislike surprises, go for an adult cross-breed.

## CROSS-BREED FASHIONS

It's not just the labradoodle that's become popular in recent years. Other cutely named 'inventions' include the cockapoo (cocker spaniel/poodle), the puggle and the poogle (pug and beagle/poodle respectively), the Jack-a-bee (Jack Russell terrier/beagle) and the schnoodle (schnauzer/poodle). Every new breed has to start somewhere, of course, and where better than with two differently-abled but already popular existing breeds? Poodles and beagles crop up more than most in these current mixes – probably because both breeds are widely respected for their generally good, sound temperaments. In addition, the close-curled, non-shedding coat of the poodle can often be tolerated by people with allergies to regular dog fur, and this quality is also sometimes found in poodle mixes, which may account, in part at least, for their popularity.

# Classes of dog

Traditionally, dogs were grouped according to the work that they did, whether they were herders, hunting dogs or guard dogs. And dogs were judged according to how good they were at their work – appearance definitely took second place to utility.

Over the last 100 years, many pedigree breeds have come to be selected more for appearance, judged against exacting breed standards, rather than how useful they are.

## WHAT'S THE HERITAGE?

Although a pedigree dog today may come from a non-working line, you should still look at the job it was bred to do originally. Generations of breeding to type aren't rubbed out quickly, and a retriever breed may still have a strong instinct to retrieve, even if its parents and its grandparents weren't working dogs. Both the US and the UK Kennel Clubs, along with the national kennel clubs of many other countries, recognize seven breed categories, as set out below.

If, having looked at the general group qualities, you still remain enthusiastic about a breed, read up on it or contact a breeder to get more details of its specific character.

Left: A classic retrieving spaniel, bred both to flush game out and to retrieve it when shot.

## Gundogs/sporting dogs

Called 'gundogs' in the UK and 'sporting dogs' in the US, this group comprises retrievers, spaniels, pointers and setters. These dogs were originally bred to flush and retrieve game, from water as well as land. The ancestry survives in many breeds, most notably the Labrador and the golden retriever, which are still strongly drawn to water. Many of the dogs most favoured for family pets are found in this group, and most need penty of exercise to stay fit. Some also fall into the late-

# BASIC INSTINCT **Individuality**

Never forget that a pedigree dog, as well as being an example of selective breeding, is also both a product of its specific environmental background, and a personality in its own right. However carefully bred to type, every kennel has seen some specimens that buck the trend – dogs who don't have the expected characteristics of their breed: timid German shepherds, Border collies that can't seem to get the hang of rounding up sheep, and relaxed, mellow Jack Russell terriers. Individuality is as strong in dogs as it is in people, and breeding, while it produces a 'best odds' for the presence of desired qualities in puppies (and the absence of unwanted ones) is never 100 per cent predictable.

maturing category, meaning that they don't start to behave like adults until they're over three years old.

Members of this group can make great pets provided that they have active, fit owners who have plenty of time for training and walks.

## Hounds

This group divides into two broad types: sighthounds and scenthounds. Sighthounds were developed to run down prey, and include some of the world's fastest dogs, such as the elegant Afghan hound and the borzoi. They need regular exercise, but it can be taken in short bursts and, provided they have the opportunity to race off-leash, sighthounds are often mellow at home. It is not usually possible to train a sighthound not to chase smaller animals.

Scenthounds were bred to hunt by tracking. This group includes the popular basset hound and beagle. Although they tend to be more heavily built than sighthounds (often with large, drop ears which are said to help to waft scent towards their nostrils), scenthounds are also often very active and have plenty of stamina. They are just as determined to pursue a scent trail as sighthounds are to chase after a glimpse of their prey, so should be kept on a leash anywhere where a lengthy pursuit could cause a problem.

Right: **The glamorous, high-maintenance coat of the Afghan hound conceals the rangy build of a very fast and functional hunting dog.**

*Right:* **Boxers are often playful and boisterous – they need plenty of training to make sure they work with their owners rather than going their own way.**

## Working

The 'work' in this group's description covers a whole range of jobs, including guarding, haulage and 'search and rescue' – and a wide range of breed types, from the rottweiler to the husky. Most working dogs are sizeable, with big personalities to match. What they have in common is plenty of power and a need for patient, consistent and persistent training. If that need is met, they can make great pets. Most are too big and too powerful for novice owners.

## Terrier

These dogs were bred to be independent, with the stamina to pursue game, from foxes to rats. Terriers are single-minded and often scrappy, and this group contains some of the most dedicated diggers (and barkers) in the canine kingdom. They're popular as pets, but can be tough to train and, while characterful, are not usually the most placid of breeds even when well trained.

## Toy

The toy breeds are companion dogs, pure and simple. As the name implies, dogs in this group range from the very small to the absolutely minute and can therefore fit in with most owners and lifestyles. Pugs, papillons, Pomeranians and Chihuahuas all fall within this category. While they can often be active, the tiny size of most toys means that they don't need large amounts of exercise. Most are intelligent and trainable. Toys can be too small and fragile (and nippy) to be good with small children, and are sometimes not robust enough for family pets. They often do best with a dedicated owner, as one-person dogs. Despite their small size, many of these breeds have great self-confidence and a well-developed sense of their own importance. It is therefore crucial to train and socialize them thoroughly to prevent them becoming pocket-sized tyrants.

*Left:* **Even dedicated terrier enthusiasts wouldn't claim that they're the most biddable dogs – but they usually have plenty of personality.**

*Below:* **The Chihuahua, best known of the toy breeds, tends to have a confidence out of all proportion to its minuscule size.**

Left: **A Border collie: one of the smartest and most trainable, but also the most active, of all breeds.**

Left: **The unmistakeable build and face of the English bulldog make for a distinctive pet.**

## Pastoral

The UK pastoral group is known in the US by the more literal title of herding dogs. These dogs were originally bred to herd everything from sheep to cows, and range from the German shepherd and the Belgian Tervuren at one end of the scale, to the Welsh corgi at the other, taking in the collies, from Border to bearded, along the way. Generally, these dogs are energetic and clever.

They make rewarding but also demanding companions, as they need exercise for both body and brain, and are definitely not sensible choices for sedentary owners. Provided they are properly trained and socialized, though, many dogs in this group can make good family pets.

## Utility/Non-sporting

The utility group, known in the US as non-sporting, pulls together a number of breeds that have little in common with one another. Whereas a dog's membership of the other groups can give a potential owner an idea of what to expect in terms of breeding history, this isn't true in the case of utility dogs. Schnauzers, poodles, shar-peis and Dalmatians are all included in this category, and each of these has a distinctive character of its own. If you're considering a dog from this group, it's best to simply research the specific breed.

## Miscellaneous, non-listed breeds

These dogs, while widely accepted as pedigree dogs, have nevertheless not passed the stringent breed recognition requirements that are necessary before inclusion in the official groupings of the kennel clubs. This is of no significance in itself – a breed as popular as the Jack Russell terrier, for example, only gained official listing very recently, and its non-listed status did nothing to impede its popularity as a pet.

If you are interested in an as-yet-unlisted breed, research it separately, as you would a dog in the utility group.

# Finding a puppy

If you've decided on a specific breed and want to raise your dog from puppyhood, your next step is to find a reputable breeder. This may not be the cheapest or the quickest way to obtain a pedigree puppy, but you will end up with a good dog.

## WHAT THE BEST BREEDERS DO

Good breeders match their breeding pairs carefully and do their best to eliminate any known genetic weaknesses (to which almost all pedigrees have some tendency). They will also be prepared to discuss with you openly the genetic health problems associated with that breed.

Responsible breeders keep puppies with the dam (mother) until they are at least eight weeks old, and use this time to begin to socialize the puppies and familiarize them with different experiences. They look after the breeding mothers carefully, ensuring they are well and strong,

and are allowed reasonable lengths of time between litters. A breeder should be able to vouch for the constitution and temperament of the mother and father of the litter.

A breeder will probably have nearly as many questions for you as you have for them. They will want to know that their puppies are going to homes where they will be looked after properly, and to owners who have an awareness of that particular breed's needs. A good breeder will also always be prepared to take back a dog, at any time in its life, if your circumstances change and, for whatever reason, you can no longer keep your pet.

Left: **Most highly bred dogs have some health issues. Many of the toy breeds find it hard to give birth to their litters naturally.**

## WHERE NOT TO BUY A PUPPY

Pet-shop puppies and breeders who advertise online or in the small ads may seem like simpler (and cheaper) options for buying a puppy.

However, buying in these more informal ways is not a good idea. You will have no guarantee of a puppy's health and nowhere to go for help if you have problems later on. Worse, these ways of selling can be covers for puppies raised in puppy farms.

These farms are run solely for profit, by using bitches as breeding machines for multiple litters and almost universally keeping their dogs in horrifyingly poor conditions. The bitches are confined in very small pens and forced to have one litter after another in uncomfortable surroundings that offer the puppies little or nothing in terms of stimulation. Apart from the ethical questions raised by puppy farms, they are unlikely to give you the healthy puppy you want.

## HOW TO FIND A BREEDER

Bear in mind that big advertisements or well-designed websites don't necessarily tell you what you want to know about a breeder. It's best to get your information from a local breed club, from your veterinarian or, best of all, from the owner of a dog you've met and know. Any of these sources is likely to give you fair, unbiased information.

If possible, approach more than one breeder (this may be easier said than done if your heart is set on an unusual breed), and be prepared to wait for your puppy; few breeders

> ### CHECKLIST
> ## Questions to ask a breeder
>
> - Are there people who've bought a dog from them that you could talk to?
> - Does the breed have any genetic problems, and if so have they had any such problems in previous litters?
> - How many breeding bitches do they have, and how many litters do they have per year?
> - Are they happy to have their dogs returned if you become unable to care for them?
> - At what age will the puppies be available to collect? Will they have been wormed and have had their first shots?
> - Are full registration papers available for all their puppies? Check online with a kennel club site or with your veterinarian to see what the papers look like to avoid being offered fakes.

will have an unspoken-for litter that just happens to be ready for you to go and see.

When you've talked on the phone, arrange a visit. If you're happy with what you see, ask the breeder if you can reserve a puppy from the next litter that's due. Unless you intend to show your dog, mention from the first that you're looking for a pet, not a show dog.

# Breed rescue societies

If you're decided on a breed but don't have your heart set on a puppy, you may find your perfect dog at a breed rescue centre. There are breed rescue societies for almost every dog breed there is, and most run care centres that offer dogs for adoption.

## WHAT IS BREED RESCUE?

Breed rescue societies and centres are essentially single-breed shelters. They're usually run by enthusiasts for that breed, and take dogs of that breed only. The dogs come from a range of sources: from situations in which the dog was abused; from owners who couldn't cope or became unable to care for their dog for other reasons; sometimes from other shelters who have sought out specialized care for a dog of that particular breed. Like the general shelters, almost all the breed rescue societies are run on a shoestring. Most, like general shelters, make a charge to anyone wanting to adopt a dog in their care. Charges tend to be slightly higher at breed rescue centres than at general shelters.

There are several advantages in adopting from a breed rescue society. First, the staff will have a full knowledge of the breed – both its advantages and its downsides. They will have had day-to-day contact with every shade of personality the breed offers (which cannot normally be said of high-end breeders). As a result, they will have a good idea of the different temperaments of the dogs in their care and may guide you towards exactly the dog you're looking for.

They will also be able to give you a warts-and-all description of the breed. While this may puncture your dream of a 'perfect' dog, it will be an excellent preparation for actually owning him. The dogs in breed

Left: **Breed centres usually keep dogs in individual pens for viewing, just as general shelters do.**

centres will also usually have been through assessment and health checks, so staff will be able to give you a fair amount of information about a particular dog.

Breed rescue societies, like shelters, very seldom have puppies, and this can be viewed as another advantage. When you look for adult dogs you can see – in terms of size and, to some extent temperament, what you would be getting.

Finally, if you adopt from a breed rescue, you'll not only have the breed you want, you'll also be able to give a homeless dog a home.

## PASSING THE ADOPTION TEST

Staff at a breed rescue centre, will be doing their utmost to place the dogs in their care permanently, but only to good homes. It surprises many would-be adopters, who see themselves as rescuers and therefore expect to be given a dog straight away, that they have to go through a screening process.

This process can be rigorous and is designed to establish whether or not you would make a suitable owner. It's precisely *because* they are rescue dogs that their temporary carers don't want them to be passed around a second time.

Although you may be asked many questions, they are not intended to put you off. The staff are simply doing their utmost to ensure that the adoption is a success and that their dog is going to a suitable home.

Some centres may even make it a requirement to visit you and the dog at your home after the adoption.

## CHECKLIST
## Questions you may be asked (and should be happy to answer)

- Will there be someone available at home with the dog all the time?
- Will the dog be living in a house with children?
- How much exercise will you give the dog? And do you live somewhere where he can be exercised off the leash?
- Do you have any other pets?
- Does your home have a garden (and, if so, what size and is it secure?)

- - - - - - - - - - - - - - - - - - - - -

Don't be afraid to ask just as many questions yourself. Staff should be happy to answer any queries you have. Bear in mind, though, that they may not always have full background information on a specific dog.

Right: **It's worth taking the time to talk to staff at the breed shelter; they'll often be a mine of information on the breed in general.**

# Shelter dogs

If you want a pet but don't mind if he has no pedigree, and you'd prefer to take on an adult dog, then try your local dog shelter first. Be warned: shelters can be a challenge for a real dog-lover as the temptation is to adopt almost all the dogs in there.

On average, three-quarters of the inhabitants of general shelters are mongrels. There also tends to be an imbalance in the ages of shelter dogs: more are adolescents or elderly than are middle-aged. The reasons for this may be that adolescent dogs are at their hardest-to-handle stage, so it's a point at which less-dedicated owners give up on them, while elderly dogs often develop expensive health problems.

Below: **Keep your key points in mind during the visit, but stay flexible about less important requirements.**

## HOW SHELTERS WORK

There are a number of different types of shelter. Some are run by dog charities, others by local authorities, while still others are organized by private individuals.

The largest may have hundreds of dogs up for adoption, the smallest just a few at any one time. Policies and rules surrounding adoptions also vary, but there are some constants.

If a dog was not already neutered or spayed when it was brought into the shelter, most organizations insist that this happens before the dog is

adopted by anyone else. Their motivation is basically to avoid more indiscriminate breeding. Some shelters will only carry out the neutering after an adopter has been found (and in some cases, they will ask you, as the dog's future owner, to pay for the procedure).

If, for any reason, you would prefer an unneutered dog you may have to produce some very good arguments to persuade the shelter to deviate from its policy.

## 'TRYING OUT' A DOG FIRST

As well as having a separate room or space where you can meet with a dog you think that you might like to adopt, many shelters allow 'try outs' for the dogs in their care. Possibilities can range from allowing you to take the dog out for a walk to overnight visits in your home, or even stays of a day or two.

These are a sensible idea, because a dog that appeared quiet and sad in the shelter may show quite another side to his character when he's out walking or at home in domestic surroundings. Some shelters also allow you a window of time after adoption during which you can bring the dog back if things don't work out. This varies, but is not usually longer than two or three weeks.

Most shelters ask for a donation before you adopt a dog. Many will stipulate a minimum amount. Don't let this prevent you giving more if you are able. Shelters are usually short of money, and most will do their absolute best for the dogs in their care.

## CHECKLIST
## How to prepare for a shelter visit

- **HARDEN YOUR HEART.** Write down your 'must haves' on a piece of paper and keep it as a reminder. It's one thing – a good thing – to stay a little flexible in your approach to finding the perfect dog, but it's quite another to come home with a dog that's twice as large and four times as active as you thought you wanted 'because he had sad eyes'.
- **GO ALONE** or with a level-headed friend or partner. Don't take anyone who will sway your own judgement. Do take someone who will remind you of what you said you wanted.
- **DON'T WAVER.** If you have a cat and the shelter staff tell you that the dog whose pen you keep returning to is unreliable with cats, don't tell yourself that you're sure they'll learn to get along together.
- **ARM YOURSELF** with a packet of small treats. If you see a dog you'd like to meet, some tasty snacks may ease your first encounter.

Above: **Offer a toy during your first meeting to gauge how strongly your dog feels about his accessories.**

## FIRST MEETING

Wait until you've walked round the whole shelter and looked at all the dogs a couple of times before you decide which – if any – you would like to meet. If you ask to meet a dog a member of staff will usually collect him and bring him to you in a room or space away from the pens.

In some shelters this space is furnished; if so, sit down and make your body language as relaxed as possible. If the dog is nervous, your relaxed posture will help him.

Usually the staff member will stay with you once the dog is in the room. Use this first encounter to take a good look at the dog. Does he approach you happily or hang back nervously? Does he look like he's in good condition?

The guide to body language in chapter one will help you 'read' how he's feeling. Don't stare at the dog or prolong eye contact. Look around you and chat to the staff member in a relaxed tone during the meeting.

Ask if you can offer the dog a treat and, if feeding is allowed, throw a treat on the floor near you (don't try to feed the dog straight from your hand). If the dog eats it eagerly and approaches you, feed him one or two more directly. If he doesn't seem nervous, you could try asking him to 'sit' for a treat. If he backs off at any point or starts barking, don't assume that this is a problem. Shelter dogs have often had limited human contact and become either over-excited or nervous with new people.

If the dog remains friendly or relaxed, pet him a little and see if he welcomes some physical contact. If you stroke him, stick to the side of the body, the chest or under the chin, and stroke gently, don't pat. Don't pat him on top of the head either (most dogs hate this) and don't put an arm around him – these are not friendly gestures in dog-talk.

## SHELTERS ONLINE

Many of the larger shelters have lists of the dogs they can offer for adoption online, together with photos and brief physical and character descriptions. If you're happy to do your research on the computer, it can save some time and give you a good overview of the range of dogs available for adoption from your local shelters. You can visit once you've narrowed down the field.

CHECKLIST
## Questions to ask about a shelter dog

If the meeting goes well and you have a good feeling about the dog, ask some questions to fill in your knowledge before you take a decision such as:

- How much do the staff know about the dog's background? Was he given up by an owner? Was he a stray, or saved from an abusive situation?
- How old is he or she? (The answer may be approximate if the dog was abandoned.)
- Has the shelter carried out a temperament assessment? What did it tell them? Most shelters make an assessment before a dog is offered for adoption; if they haven't, or don't assess any dogs, it's not the sign of a good shelter. Ask if an assessment can be done; if the answer is still 'no', then consider going to another shelter.

- Is there one particular member of staff who has worked closely with the dog? If so, would it be possible to discuss the dog with them?
- Is the dog good with other dogs? Is he friendly with children?
- Has the dog shown signs of aggression since he was brought into the shelter?
- What is the dog's state of health? Has he had any medication since being brought into the shelter? All shelter dogs are examined by a veterinarian when they arrive so you can find out if he has any serious health problems.

## AFTER THE MEETING

The shelter may require that someone visits you in your home before you can adopt a dog. If you have other pets, you should ask to take the dog home overnight to see if they'll get on together. And, even if you've been assured by shelter staff that the dog is fine with kids, it's crucial that dog and children meet before you finalize arrangements and that they are careful and respectful with him. Unless you're absolutely certain you have found the right dog, go home and sleep on it before making your final decision.

Right: Shelter staff may not have much time for grooming; your scruffy selection may effect a Cinderella-like transformation when he gets the full at-home grooming treatment.

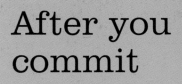

# After you commit

You've chosen your dog, whether it's a puppy from a breeder, a breed rescue, or a mongrel from the local shelter. Now it's time to confirm your choice and fix a date to collect him. Plan ahead to make the journey and homecoming as easy as possible.

## FROM A BREEDER

Many breeders have waiting lists, so it may be some months since you reserved a puppy from the breeder's next litter. Puppies usually go off to their new homes at around eight weeks of age.

If the breeder is some distance away, don't forget to set up the car for the journey with items such as a puppy crate, a couple of clean old towels or blankets and some wet wipes for accidents.

An experienced breeder won't have fed the puppy on the morning of his first car journey, and it's best to wait to give him food until you get back home, or you'll be virtually guaranteeing carsickness. Your puppy may be sick anyway, so have a spare clean towel to hand so that you can clean him up and make him comfortable again if you've still got some distance to go.

If it's going to be a journey of an hour or two, it's a good idea to bring a water bottle and a small puppy bowl so that he can have a drink on the way.

CHECKLIST
**Picking up a puppy from a breeder**

**Before leaving with your puppy, do the following:**

- Ask for the registration papers for your pet.
- Ask for notes of the puppy's first shots and worming. You'll need these for your first veterinarian's appointment.
- Check the details of what the puppy is eating, how often, and in what quantities. Most breeders will give you a prepared sheet but if not, ask.
- Ask if you can have something that smells familiar to help the puppy settle in. Many breeders will give you something like a blanket that's been in the puppy pen or a soft toy that will smell of 'home' to your puppy.

## FROM A SHELTER

Circumstances in shelters change quickly, so you may not have as much time to prepare for a shelter dog as you would if you were collecting from a breeder. When you collect your dog don't overwhelm him with attention immediately. Keep your tone happy and calm when you're talking to him, and bring a leash to the shelter when you go to collect him (many shelter dogs wear collars anyway, so he may already have one – check before you arrive and, if not, ask for his collar size so that you can bring a collar with you). Just as you would with a puppy, ask if the shelter has a blanket or a toy that you can take home with you. They won't always have anything, but if they can give you something it'll help your dog to feel that things around him are familiar at a time of change.

## MORE THAN ONE DOG?

If you're introducing a new dog to a household where there is a pet already, go gently. If you're bringing a puppy home to share space with an older, easygoing dog you will probably find that they'll work out their relationship comparatively quickly.

Supervise their time together – don't leave them alone until it's clear that they're used to each other. If you need to go out, you can put the puppy in a separate room or in a playpen away from your older dog. Prepare yourself not to interfere when the established dog corrects the puppy, provided that the correction is appropriate, and not over-aggressive. Make sure that your older dog is

Above: **A careful introduction gives your old and new dogs the best chance of becoming good friends.**

given plenty of attention and that his own patterns are disrupted as little as possible.

If you're bringing an adult dog home, it's best for the dogs to meet first outside the house. Ideally you should visit the shelter and bring the dog you want to adopt on one or two outings with your existing pet so that you can see how they get along. If all goes well, on adoption day, arrange for them to meet outside and take them out before bringing them back home together.

This gentle introduction should minimize problems. Plan things so that you can supervise their time with each other until they're obviously getting along well. Feed them in separate spots for a while, too, to ensure that resource-guarding aggression doesn't crop up around the food bowl. You might want to put away your dog's favourite toys for a little while, too, and give each dog a new toy or two of its own.

# Preparing your home

Whether you're getting a puppy or an adult dog, it's best to pet-proof the house before you bring him home, rather than afterwards. That way it'll be easier to enjoy your first few days with the new member of the family.

Even if you already have pets, you'll need to take some extra care with a new dog until you know what his habits are; whether these are chewing electric flexes or rolling on the bed.

With a puppy, the main issues you'll be dealing with in the first few weeks are likely to be house training and chewing. With an adult dog, particularly if you don't know much about his background, the teething problems are less predictable – although hopefully house training won't be one of them.

Consider where you want your new pet to spend his time before rearranging anything you need to accommodate him. You can install child-gates to confine a dog, puppy or adult, to specific parts of the house if you want. Even if you plan eventually to give him the run of the house, you may opt to keep him in certain rooms (kitchen, utility room, hall) while you're getting to know one another, and especially while you're out.

Right: **If your puppy is loose around the house, line his pen and the floor with paper.**

## PUPPY PROOFING

In theory, we know that puppies love to chew. In practice, few owners are prepared for quite how voracious the chewing urge can be. Go through the house removing everything chewable from the floor and shutting it away, from books to shoes and bags (anything that is leather is always a favourite for a teething puppy).

Right: **Child-proof gates can be useful for confining a new dog to certain parts of the house when you can't keep an eye on him.**

Just as important, stock up on chew toys so that you'll be ready to give the puppy something he *can* chew. These should be made from hard rubber or rawhide, so that they either won't come to pieces or (with rawhide) are safe to swallow. Store away electric flexes as far as possible, and get into the habit of unplugging and switching off when you're leaving a room. Don't forget that adult dogs can have a chewing habit, too, so plan in the same way for a new adult dog. You can relax the rules if you find that he limits his chewing to his own possessions.

Set up a safe space for the puppy for when you're busy or not in a room. Even if you're planning to crate-train him (see page 80), there will be times when you can't keep an eye on him that are too long for confinement in a crate.

Either puppy proof a room (no flexes, no houseplants, no breakables or chewables within height range; cleaning materials or other harmful chemicals put away in a dog-proof cupboard; a layer of old newspaper underfoot), so that he can stay there for a while with the door closed, or alternatively, get a child's play pen so you can put him in there when you don't have time to watch him.

## OUTDOORS

Check that any outside space you have is dog-proof. Fill or block holes in any hedging or fencing (even quite small holes). There have been cases of small but energetic breeds scaling formidable fences, so err on the side of caution.

If you've chosen a breed that likes to dig – terriers in particular are talented in this area – consider installing chicken wire along your garden boundaries. It may not stop your dog, but it should slow him down long enough for someone to notice what he's doing.

Check with your veterinarian about plants that are poisonous if eaten. Few adult dogs will eat outdoor plants but some do, and puppies will chew on leaves.

# A new puppy: what to expect

Like those of a new baby, a puppy's needs are both basic and fairly constant. You're now set up with the food bowls, the collar and leash, the crate, basket and puppy toys. But you may find it hard to imagine what daily life with a puppy entails.

## PLAYING AND SLEEPING

Puppies play hard and they get tired quickly. One moment your new arrival will be zooming around like a hyperactive fly, the next he'll be fast asleep. Puppies need their rest as well as their exercise, so warn any children in the household that when the puppy wants to sleep, he should be left alone.

Puppies are always amusing to play with, but even at eight weeks there are good and bad ways to play (see pages 84–5 for guidelines on puppy handling). A nippy puppy can grow up into a biting adult, and vigorous bouts of play wrestling may not be as much fun with a grown dog. Getting your puppy to chase after you is good (better preparation for training than you chasing him), and most dogs enjoy a game of tug. Buy a couple of toys for his arrival; you can add more when you see what he likes.

## FEEDING

The breeder, or shelter, will give you guidelines on what your puppy has been eating up to now. Stick to the same diet for the first week or two to avoid stomach upsets. You may be feeding him as many as four meals a day at first and the feeding schedule you've been given should also tell you at what age you can start to give fewer, larger meals. If you're bringing

Below: **Puppies play and sleep with equal intensity; you may find he doesn't wake even if you pick him up.**

a puppy into a household in which there's already an older dog, feed the adult at the same time as you feed the puppy. Divide the amount your older dog usually gets into smaller meals, and put his meal down first, in a corner away from the puppy.

## HOUSE TRAINING

House training a puppy can take a while or a long while (that's weeks or months), but you should always begin as soon as you get home.

Set up a room for the puppy that has a washable floor. You can put down layers of newspaper to help with the clearing up. Persistence and positive reinforcement are the keys to house training. Every time the puppy wakes from a nap or finishes a meal, take him outside – these are the likeliest times for him to want to go. Ignore accidents but praise him lavishly whenever he's successful. Never punish a puppy for peeing indoors. If you catch him in the act, take him outdoors as quickly as you can and praise him if he manages to pee, even a little, outside.

One house-training method suggests that you train the puppy to eliminate onto sheets of newspaper or special 'training pads' placed on the floor, and then move the paper nearer and nearer the door until it's outside. This may turn house-training into a two-stage process (the puppy learns to 'go' on the paper, and only later to go outside), so it won't necessarily speed things up, but it may cut down on the amount of floor-mopping you have to do in the meantime.

# An adult dog: what to expect

If you're adopting an adult, try to learn as much as you can about his background. If shelter staff can't give you much detail – for example, if the dog was a stray – ask to take him out for walks and home visits before you commit to adopting him.

When you don't know what previous experiences your dog has had, it can be helpful to have some knowledge of canine body language. It will make it easier for you to tell if he's feeling fearful/playful/aggressive/nervous.

Read up on dog behaviour (see chapter one, and some of the suggested titles in the reading list on page 188) before adoption day. You should also look at ways to send reassuring signs with your own body language. You can send calming signals to a dog by relaxing your posture as well as by talking soothingly to him.

Below: **Wait until you've had your dog a little while before introducing raw bones; he may become very possessive of such a valuable treat.**

## ASSESSMENTS AND BEHAVIOUR

A responsible shelter will have passed your dog as fit for adoption when they assessed him. Ask what the process involved: some centres introduce each new dog to a variety of different people, including children, when they're trying to judge what sort of home he would fit into, while other assessments are more basic. However thorough the shelter was, you can never really tell how a dog will behave in domestic surroundings until you get him home and see how he adjusts to day-to-day living across the course of a few weeks. Experienced dog carers tell adopters that the first fortnight or so is the grace period with an adopted dog, and that engrained habits, good or bad, tend only to emerge when the dog is beginning to feel safe in familiar surroundings.

Unless they have never lived indoors – in which case, you'll probably have to start with the house training from scratch, as you would with a puppy – most adult dogs will

be house trained, and many will have had other basic training and be able to sit, stay, walk on the leash and so on. Over the first few days be observant while you're out walking your dog. If you don't know if he'll come back to you, exercise him on a long leash and see how he gets on with other dogs out and around.

Practise throwing a ball or Frisbee in an enclosed space (if you don't have a large garden, a local ball court out-of-hours is ideal) to see if he's a natural retriever. See how he is at the front door, first with a single visitor, then with two or three visitors at a time: gradually build on his experiences, bit by bit, until you find what his limits are.

If you're lucky – as thousands of adopters are – you'll find that you have a nice dog that fits in with your lifestyle, gets along well with other

**Above:** Take a new adult dog out and around to see how he behaves in various different environments.

dogs, loves his toys and enjoys meeting new people. Even if the gradual approach brings to light a few problems, most can be fixed.

## TRAINING SESSIONS
Basic training and socialization glitches are often solved simply by attending dog-training classes. Trickier behaviour, such as on-leash aggression or over-enthusiastic resource-guarding, are best tackled with one-on-one sessions with a professional behaviourist, who can usually both explain what causes the behaviour and suggest ways of amending it. While consultations aren't cheap, just one or two sessions are often enough to give you the key to solving the problem behaviour.

# First days with a new arrival

Take time out to be fairly constantly around the house for the first few days after your new dog arrives. If you're house training a puppy, you'll need to be around for much longer than that as you'll need to spot the right moment to put him outdoors.

Even for an adult, housetrained dog, you have to set up a routine, reinforce housetraining and basic obedience if necessary, and begin to accustom your pet to everyday life in your house, from the sound of the vacuum cleaner to the layout of the garden. That's not to say you should smother him with attention. Spend plenty of time walking with him, playing with him and having fun, but carry on your usual day around him too – the sooner he gets settled in, the sooner he will feel secure.

If you've taken on an adult dog, use this initial period to see how often he needs to go out. Middle-aged dogs tend to have better bladder control than very young or elderly ones, and it's part of your job as owner to make sure that your dog gets out when he needs to.

If your grown-up dog has a few accidents, be patient and use positive reinforcement to stress that he should go outdoors; it may mean either that he's a bit confused or that you're leaving overlong intervals between trips out.

## AGREE THE RULES

Set up some rules that everyone in the household agrees to enforce (if you have kids, hold a family meeting about this to make sure that everyone gets the idea). There's no right or wrong to the rules you set up. Some people are happy to let their dog on the furniture, for example, while others are not.

Left: **Home comforts – consistency matters more to your dog than what the house rules are.**

## BASIC INSTINCT **When dogs meet cats**

In general, cats and dogs can get along if they are introduced carefully. Always supervise the first few encounters between a cat and a dog, and make sure the dog approaches the cat with caution (a cat's claws can do more than just frighten an unprepared puppy). Have the dog on a leash when they first meet so that he can't chase the cat if the meeting doesn't go to plan, and ask him to sit to give the cat the chance to make an approach if it wants to. Talk to the dog in a soothing voice while the cat's around, keeping at least some of his attention on you, and make sure he'll be under your control if the cat runs away – you need to ensure that he can't act on his chase impulse. Your cat must have plenty of dog-free spaces to go to if they don't take to each other immediately. While cats and dogs are occasionally good friends, more commonly they co-exist and largely ignore one another. Feed them in separate places, and make sure that the dog can't steal the cat's food – if necessary, put it out of reach on a surface that the cat can reach but the dog can't.

What's important is that if your dog is allowed on the furniture he's *always* allowed on the furniture, while if he isn't, he *never* is. Dogs understand and are reassured by consistency, and it isn't fair to expect your pet to follow different sets of rules with different family members.

## NIGHT ROUTINES

Most breeders and trainers recommend that a new dog is kept close to where you sleep at first. Puppies will need to be let out last thing at night and first thing in the morning, and usually once or twice during the night too. Ideally you should put the puppy's or dog's crate in your room, set it up cosily with a blanket and perhaps a soft toy, and then shut your puppy in.

Some people put a hot-water bottle in with a new puppy to emulate the warmth of his mother for the first night or two. If you want to do this, wrap it up well in towels or a blanket, so that it can't be chewed, and fill it with hot rather than boiling water. Don't weaken and take the puppy out at the first whimper, and definitely don't allow him on the bed with you.

Time two outside breaks at even intervals through the night. You can set an alarm clock for these, but it's likely that your puppy will whine loudly and wake you up when he really needs to go out – although he may have one or two accidents at first; small puppies have very little bladder control. Take him outside, give him a minute or two, praise him warmly if he performs, then put him straight back in his crate. An older dog may not be used to or happy with a crate – if you find that he settles down more easily in a basket, give him that instead (see pages 80–1).

# Basic dog care

You've chosen your dog and brought him home. Now you need to work out how you're going to live together, just as you would with any new relationship. To a great extent dogs, both as puppies and as adults, want the same things that humans do: to feel safe, to be fed and warm, and to enjoy the company of those around them. The difference between us is that while we humans can sort most things out for ourselves, our dogs are dependent on us to provide for them.

This chapter looks at the practicalities of running your dog's life day to day. It takes you through the basics, from what to expect at your first visit to the veterinarian to socialization exercises for a puppy or a shy adult dog. It covers all the feeding options – plus grooming and bathing routines. Remember, the habits you establish now will last throughout your dog's life, which could be anything from seven years to fifteen, or more. It's worth taking the time to set up a lifestyle that your dog will thrive on, that works for you and that will keep you both happy.

# A place to sleep

Where your dog sleeps will be important to him, and you need to make an arrangement that fits in with your living space too. What this is depends on the age, size and type of dog you have and on the personal preference of both you and your pet.

### USING A DOG CRATE

Over the last two decades the popularity of crates in which dogs can rest and sleep (and sometimes be confined in while their owners are out) has grown enormously. If you're a traditionalist, who grew up with a family dog that slept in a basket in a corner of the kitchen, a crate may jar with your vision of dog care.

Basically, it's a box with a front door that can be fixed closed, and it's usually made either entirely from wire mesh or has plastic panels with a mesh door. A puppy that is carefully introduced to his crate usually becomes very attached to it, seeing it as a comfortable den to which he can retreat when he wants to sleep or if he simply wants some downtime.

Many owners also use crates to confine dogs safely during car journeys and, in a busy household, a new pet can be usefully placed in a crate so as to be out from underfoot

for a short while. A crate can also be a handy aid for house training a puppy, as he will be disinclined to soil the space where he sleeps – if he is kept inside his crate for a brief time he will be encouraged to 'hold on' until he can get outside.

### THE ALTERNATIVES

Crates aren't for every dog. They're usually impractical for the very largest breeds, and some dogs never grow to like them. Shelter dogs, in particular, can have a problem with them, if in the life before you owned them they were left in them for too

Right: **Comfortable bedding and, if possible, a familiar blanket, will help to accustom your dog to his crate.**

long, and so associate them with loneliness. If you have a calm dog who isn't destructive while you are out, you may see no need for one – in this case, the basket in the kitchen may be the right choice. Even if you don't choose to use a crate at home, it is useful to have one for travelling and staying in other people's houses. If you're a novice dog-owner try one first: dogs often like them and you may never look back.

If you don't want to use a crate, give some thought to where your dog is going to sleep long term. Some dogs sleep in a basket during the day and alongside their owners on the bed at night. (If this is your preference, consider carefully about whether you'll be as happy about it when your sweet German shepherd puppy is all grown-up). If you have a dog that you're not confident about disciplining, make sure he sleeps in his own space, not yours.

If you opt for a basket, the easiest type to keep is made from hard plastic or woven cane, and lined with a washable blanket or cushion. If you choose one of the all-fabric padded options, check that it's washable before you buy.

## CHECKLIST
## Crate etiquette

### Do

🐾 Buy a crate that is big enough. Your dog should be able to turn around easily and to lie down in it with his legs stretched out.

🐾 Make the crate inviting. Line it with a comfortable blanket and leave toys and treats in it regularly.

🐾 Introduce a puppy or dog to a crate gradually. Make sure he is used to going in and out of it before you shut the door for the first time.

🐾 Keep the door shut for very short periods – just five or ten minutes at first – until your dog is relaxed about staying in his crate for longer.

### Don't

🐾 Keep a crate your puppy has outgrown. If it isn't big enough, you need to replace it.

🐾 Force a dog into his crate or shut him in when he isn't familiar with it. It's frightening for the dog and he may develop a phobia about being shut in.

🐾 Leave your dog in his crate for long periods. Crates are for sleeping in or for keeping your pet safely for short periods. No dog should be left shut in a crate for hours on end.

🐾 Leave a puppy in a crate after he has soiled it. Crated puppies should be checked at short, regular intervals. If the crate needs cleaning, do it straight away. Never speak sharply to your puppy or punish him for making a mess in his crate.

# A safe space

If your new dog is an adult, you may want to wait to see how he settles over the first few days before deciding on the best place in the house to make his space. If he's reasonably house trained, you'll be able to allow him some freedom to explore.

Even a young and playful adult dog is unlikely to be as energetic and as into everything as a puppy, so you can be a little more relaxed than you would be with a puppy.

Take the decision whether you want to use a crate or not, and if you do, prepare to be very patient about getting him to go in it. If he wasn't crate-trained when he was very young, you may find that he's more crate-averse than you would expect a new puppy to be.

Use treats and toys, not coercion, and if he shows anxiety, leave the door open, rewarding him when he goes into it with more treats and praise (make sure you time this right, rewarding at the moment he goes into the crate, not at the moment he is thinking of coming out of it). Some new owners even feed their new dog his meals in his crate to ramp up the positive associations.

## SETTING UP A SPACE

If you don't feel strongly about crate training your adult dog, set up a space for him in a quiet corner, not too near the main traffic through the house – a corner of the kitchen or hall is often best. Make it cosy with a basket and blankets. If you are buying a new basket, bear in mind that many rescue dogs like beds with sides. They seem to prefer a spot that feels more protected than other 'open' resting options,

Left: **Dogs need a space where they can feel safe so put the basket in a quiet corner and make it warm and comfortable.**

such as thick padded cushions or beanbags – you could take your pet with you when you shop for his basket to gauge his particular preference. Set his water bowl nearby and put a couple of toys and chews in the basket too.

You may find that he goes to 'his' corner automatically when he wants to relax or is finding the household a bit too busy for him, but if he doesn't, you can encourage him to 'go in your corner' with a treat or a chew toy.

## TALKING TO YOUR PET

Most human owners talk to their pets a lot. Talking, after all, is what humans do. Don't underestimate the value of quiet time with your new dog, though. A young, responsive dog in particular may be looking to you constantly, at first for signals as to what he 'should' be doing, and the very fact that you're talking in his direction can increase his alertness as he tries to understand what's expected of him.

Of course this varies from breed to breed and according to a dog's particular personality, but some periods of judicious silence will let your dog know that he doesn't have to be on full alert all the time at home. And if you just can't stop yourself talking, keep your tone low and soothing rather than high with a lot of questioning notes. Save the enthusiastic, rising tone for when you really want your dog to do something.

Below: **A soft toy that can be mouthed is often a popular option for your dog to have in his basket or crate.**

## BASIC INSTINCT **Re-focusing an adult dog**

Positive reinforcement – praise for doing something right – doesn't seem to come as naturally to us when we're training our dogs as negative feedback does when he does something wrong. If you're tempted to tell your dog 'no!' for the hundredth time that day, remember that dogs are living in a non-canine environment. The best motivation you can give them for doing something that doesn't come naturally (walking on a leash, sitting down rather than chasing that squirrel) is to give the unnatural behaviour a strong association with something good (a treat and praise). For the same reason, the best way to stop a dog from doing something you don't want him to do is to redirect him towards something you *do* want him to do, which he knows from past experience will have a payoff for him. It's especially important to remember this when you're dealing with an adult dog that may not have had consistent treatment up to now. If you're trying to re-train him, his associations with you should all be positive to get the best results.

# Handling a puppy

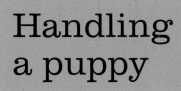

How a puppy is handled physically during its first few months will determine how it responds to being handled when it's older. A timid dog can be made fearful by rough or insensitive treatment, while a bold one can get into the habit of nipping.

Animal behaviourists believe that the 'window' during which dogs are most strongly influenced by the circumstances and events around them occurs at between four and 16 weeks. Since most puppies are brought to their new homes at around eight weeks old, this means that their first two months with you are crucial to the way they develop later. So it's a good idea to handle your puppy frequently during those first few weeks – and, just as important, to do it in the right way.

## TESTING A PUPPY

One of the tests that behaviourists and veterinarians sometimes carry out on small puppies to assess personality is to hold the puppy on its back with a hand, restraining it gently when it tries to get up. A 'soft' puppy may wriggle a little and then relax against the pressure, while a more bullish puppy may continue to push quite hard against the restraint. All puppies should learn to be tolerant of being gently handled. The more yours works against restraint, the

more crucial it is that you get him used to it early on. At some point in his life, your dog is likely be touched intrusively by someone who doesn't have a good understanding of canine language. It's at these moments that his early acclimatization will pay off, when he can show that he is prepared to put up with things that he doesn't like, because he holds humans in a position of trust.

## BASIC INSTINCT
### Learning to accept handling

To a puppy, it seems rude and unnatural to be handled in the ways you need to use to teach restraint. But you're working towards his acceptance that if he lets you do what you want, he won't be hurt, and he will be freed from the restraint exercise if he doesn't resist you. That's a valuable lesson for you to teach even a small puppy, and it's one that will be rewarded handsomely when he's a full-grown dog.

## TEACHING RESTRAINT

Areas of sensitivity in most dogs are paws, ears and mouth. Although there are always exceptions to the rule, very few dogs enjoy being held or examined in these areas. Practise restraint training exercises to get him accustomed to being held in ways he doesn't like. You don't have to cover all the sensitive points every time, but try to get him to accept at least one in each handling session. Keep the sessions short, and end them on a positive note by playing with your puppy for a minute or two.

Above: **Give children ground rules for handling a puppy so that they don't encourage bad habits.**

## CHECKLIST
### Restraint training exercises

- Start by either holding the puppy on your knee or sitting alongside him. Stroke him all over with long, gentle strokes. Don't tap or pat him; simply stroke his whole body.
- When he's relaxed, pick up one of his paws. A dog's natural instinct will be to pull away. Keep holding the paw. If the dog is wriggling, don't keep turning it over or exerting pressure – just contain it lightly in your hand while stroking him with your other hand, until he starts to relax. As soon as you feel him relax, even infinitesimally, release his paw. Try this with each paw in turn, front and back. Never release the paw until the puppy starts to relax, but be quick – let him go at the instant he stops resisting you. This will teach him not to feel threatened by your touch.

- When you've finished with the paws, repeat the process with his ears. Lift the ears, run your fingers around the edges of the ear and the ear flap. Again, if he pulls his head away, keep your fingers in place. As soon as he relaxes, remove them.
- After the ears, try his mouth. Don't lay your hand over his nose, or try to prise his mouth open. Instead, gently run your finger inside his upper lip near the corner of his mouth. As you move up towards the 'fang' tooth (the large incisor), try to slip your finger into his mouth and open it gently. If your puppy resists, keep holding him, but don't pull against him. As with all the exercises, as soon as he relaxes, let him go.

# Socializing your puppy

Socialization is key to the development of a happy, well-behaved adult dog, and socializing a puppy thoroughly is the best way of giving him a good start in life. You can continue the process that was begun naturally amongst his brothers and sisters.

A carefully socialized puppy becomes an adult that is open to new experiences, expects the best from every encounter and can take setbacks and frustrations in his stride. While it won't necessarily solve major behavioural problems, timely socialization can go a long way towards ensuring that they don't arise. It can even help you to overcome minor glitches in a puppy's nature: if he's shy, it will convince him that new things needn't be worrying; if he's a little bold and pushy, it will modify his over-boisterous approaches when they may not be appropriate.

## WHAT IS SOCIALIZATION?

'Socialization' is simply a blanket term for introducing your new dog to a wide range of experiences and loading them with positive associations. It doesn't mean overwhelming a puppy with every experience possible, without any management on your part.

Constant new experiences should become part of a puppy's life from eight weeks, at which time he's usually separated from his family, up until the 16-week mark, which behaviourists believe ends the period during which dogs learn fastest and most about the outside world.

Below: **Persuading your dog to try new experiences should be a family effort that starts young.**

Left: Rewarding your puppy for good behaviour rather than punishing him for mistakes teaches him that you are the source of his most valued experiences.

## SOCIALIZATION AND IMMUNIZATION

Many breeders and veterinarians suggest that new owners don't take puppies out and about before they've had their last immunity shots (these are usually given at 18 weeks; see pages 92–3). Because his immunity may be compromised before then, a new puppy shouldn't be around dogs that may not have been fully immunized, or be allowed to sniff around in places that are frequented by a large number of other dogs, such as parks or regular dog-walking spots. Don't let this interfere with your puppy's socialization.

A good way around the need for caution is to ask well behaved adult dogs over for play dates with your puppy, to give him the chance to meet different dogs in familiar surroundings. Many veterinarians also hold 'puppy parties', at which a group of owners with puppies of a similar age meet up so that the puppies can mix and play together.

## HOW TO MANAGE NEW EXPERIENCES

While they may be happy to take their puppy out and about, some owners question how they can 'manage' situations that they feel are outside their control.

The answer is to be selective – and also to create some situations if they don't arise naturally. Socializing means widening your dog's range of experiences, not exposing him to any experience possible.

During these first few months, keep a pocketful of treats when you're around your puppy. Give them to adults and children to pass to your puppy to give him positive associations about meeting new people. Get them to throw the treat a little away from them: if your dog is timid, this gives him the positive association of the treat, without forcing him to deal simultaneously with an interaction that makes him nervous.

Above: **Wherever you are, if your puppy is experiencing something new, keep the mood cheerful and upbeat.**

If you're using treats to give your pet positive associations, try to time it right. This is easier when you're dealing with a person than with a sound or an event. For instance, it's easy enough to ask the postman to give your puppy a treat if he seems to find men in uniform intimidating. It's harder to time a treat to coincide with what your dog perceives as a scary noise. If a noise does startle your dog, you can make a positive comment and immediately treat him.

Experts reckon that you have a maximum of one second if you want to link two things – event and outcome – in a dog's mind, so you have to be fast. Take your dog on outings in which you're focusing entirely on his socialization, rather than combining such an outing with a busy, errand-based trip.

## DON'T OVERDO IT

When you're trying to convince your dog that a particular person or situation is not a threat, be generous with your praise and treats, but don't treat or praise your dog for no good reason, as this will devalue the payoff for you both. You need to learn, too, to keep your body language and your tone relaxed and positive even when you're slightly nervous of what your dog may do. When he looks to you for guidance you want him to see someone who is sure of what they're doing and sure of what he will do.

This means that if you're talking, your tone should be confident, and that if he's on a leash, you're holding it loosely, not pulling on your puppy's neck, which is a sure signal to him that there's something wrong.

## WHEN THINGS GO WRONG

Despite your best efforts, your puppy may have some negative experiences. What should you do, for example, if an older dog comes for a visit and he loses his temper and, before anyone has time to intervene, gives the puppy a bite on the muzzle? First, keep calm. Don't assume your puppy is traumatized. If he's upset but the situation has calmed down, ask both dogs to sit (slightly apart) and give each a treat (if things aren't calm, put the dogs in different rooms).

Make it clear that you're in charge – of the other dog as well as your own. See how the next meeting goes (with this or any other dog) and monitor the situation carefully. Take any and every opportunity to make it clear that you are the boss.

### CHECKLIST
### Key experiences for your puppy

Even if you have to make special trips or arrange 'happenings', try to make sure that before your puppy is 16 weeks old, he has experienced the following:

- A car journey. Ideally, he should go on a short bus or train journey too.
- A walk near traffic, on a leash.
- Visits to various homes.
- Introductions to a wide range of people, both adults and children, carrying a wide range of props, from bicycles to hats and walking sticks. You can enlist the postman, meter reader, etc., to accustom him to uniforms.
- A walk in the countryside.
- The opportunity to mix with as many other dogs as possible, both on and off the leash. If necessary, you can create this situation artificially, with dogs you know are friendly and easy-going.
- The sight of livestock – cows, sheep, horses – from a little distance away.
- Loud noises, such as fireworks, thunderstorms and cars backfiring.

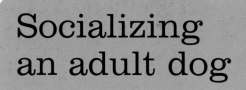

# Socializing an adult dog

Plenty of dogs that are adopted as adults adjust into their new homes easily and with the minimum of fuss. Others have a few behavioural problems which, if tackled sensibly, are easily fixed. Just a few have serious problems that require professional help.

Whichever category your adopted pet falls into, it's important to learn as much about him as you can and to spend plenty of time interacting with him in the first few weeks. Just as you would with a puppy, keep introducing him to a range of different experiences to see how he handles them.

## WATCH AND LEARN

As he begins to settle in with you, spend time observing your dog and reading his behaviour. If he came from a shelter and nobody knew much about him, don't assume that he had a bad or abusive background.

There are so many stories about mistreated dogs that it can be easy for an owner to want to coddle a new dog, making up to him for an imagined unlucky beginning in life (some veterinarians even have a name for this: Poor Thing Syndrome). While some rescue dogs have had a hard time, plenty of others are confident, and may take advantage of an owner keen to be especially loving and gentle with a traumatized pet.

Just like a puppy, your new dog needs to find his feet and his place in the household that has consistent rules and you as his leader. After the initial week or two – the honeymoon period, during which you may be given a rather muted version of his

Left: **Plenty of exercise and play will help your dog connect with you and settle in to his new routine.**

true personality – you'll know whether your dog has any unresolved socialization problems and can begin to sort them out.

## COMMON PROBLEMS

The most common problems with adult dogs put before behaviourists are dog–dog aggression, separation anxiety and over-shyness, which can lead a dog to respond to situations with fear-based aggression when he is pressurized.

If a dog has learned a response or formed a particular behaviour in puppyhood, it may be harder to correct it once that dog is an adult but this is rarely impossible. Even if an issue can't be resolved entirely, it can usually be modified to the point at which it's merely a quirk rather than a real problem.

Bad cases of any of these three, and in particular dog–dog aggression and separation anxiety, are best

## WARNING

If a dog has bitten either another dog or a person, consult a behaviourist as soon as possible, even if the bite was minor. A dog bite can be serious and you cannot risk the possibility of it happening again.

tackled with some professional back-up. Get a recommendation from your veterinarian if you decide you need help from a trainer or a behaviourist, and check that the practitioner recommended uses only positive reinforcement, and does not believe in forceful correction (which can make a problem worse). Most behaviour modification consists of distracting the dog from the cause of the unwanted behaviour, redirecting his attention back to you, then giving him something else to think about.

## BASIC INSTINCT **Keeping things calm**

When you're dealing with a fearful or incompletely socialized adult dog, it can help to learn how to project calm yourself. Keep your vocal tone even and quite slow, and concentrate on relaxing your body language. Dogs may not be able to talk, but they're far more alert to visual signs than we are, and will be highly aware of any tension that you convey (sometimes when you're not even aware of it yourself). You could even adopt some of the dog–dog calming signs that you came across earlier

(see page 24) although you will find the tongue flick, like the play bow, is tough for humans to master! There's some evidence that yawning, turning your body at a slightly oblique angle and using 'look aways' (rather than glancing directly at a dog) are recognized by dogs as non-confrontational signals even when they're being sent by a human. If your dog is afraid of new people, consider enlisting helpers to send these body-language pointers to your dog, as well as trying them out yourself.

# Visiting the veterinarian

Schedule a visit to the veterinarian for a day or two after you get your new dog. If you need to find a local practice, a word-of-mouth recommendation is usually best: ask an owner you know, or get a name from your local shelter or a breeder.

When you make the appointment, find out what you are expected to bring. The veterinarian will want to see any notes relating to your dog's vaccine history and will also ask about any worming treatments he has had. If you have a pure-bred puppy, take his breed papers, and if the breeder supplied you with any notes or certificates showing that your puppy's stock had been screened

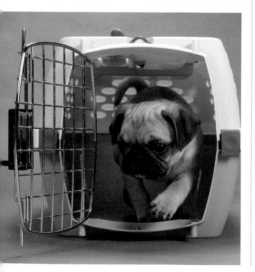

for any health conditions, bring them too. Some veterinarians also ask for a stool sample.

If you have adopted an adult dog, be ready with any information relating to his health that the pet shelter was able to tell you.

## GETTING THERE

A carrying crate is the best way to take your puppy to the veterinarian. He shouldn't be free to sniff around in the surgery, where there may be or have been sick or unvaccinated animals. If you don't have a crate, carry him. If it's your first visit with an adult dog, arm yourself with some treats. Although some older dogs don't enjoy veterinarian visits, it's usually because they bring up connections with unpleasant past experiences, other gregarious types enjoy the opportunity for a visit. If your dog belongs to the first group, be upbeat and firm with him, rather than taking a consolatory, 'poor you'

Left: **A travel crate will make managing your pet's first veterinarian experience easier.**

Above: Let your veterinarian know if your dog isn't happy being handled. He may opt to use a muzzle.

tone, as this is usually more reassuring to a fearful dog. In the waiting room, ask your dog to sit and keep him on a short leash. You don't know the other dogs there, so this isn't an ideal opportunity for socializing.

## WHAT TO EXPECT

The veterinarian will examine your puppy or dog all over. If you have a puppy, he will be checked for any sign of an umbilical hernia, a condition whereby the umbilicus has failed to close fully. The veterinarian will also establish that your dog's heart and lungs are working properly. This includes checking for a heart murmur, a condition that can be very serious.

The veterinarian will look at your dog's eyes and ears, check that he is free from parasites, look at the condition of his coat and assess whether he's in good shape. When the physical exam is over, you'll be able to ask any questions you have.

# Feeding your puppy

Like us, dogs thrive on an appropriate diet with the right balance of nutrients. However, just what constitutes an appropriate diet is the subject of numerous debates between nutritionists, veterinarians and other professionals.

There isn't even a consensus over whether dogs are omnivores or carnivores. While a majority believe that dogs are omnivores on the grounds that wild dogs eat not only meat but whatever else they can get that is palatable, there's a second group who maintain that dogs are pure carnivores on the basis of their jaw development. What is certain is that it's worth finding the diet that suits your dog: one that keeps him

healthy and which doesn't cause him digestive problems. Exactly what that diet is will depend on the dog.

## EARLY DAYS

In domestic dogs, the weaning process usually begins when they are between three and four weeks old. Breeders will start to introduce small dishes of puppy food mixed with formula milk into the puppy pen around this time and gradually the puppies will experiment with it and begin to eat some solids. By the time you get your puppy he will probably be eating four or five small meals per

Below: **Your puppy will already be on a meal plan containing solids by the time you bring him home.**

day, which may consist of branded puppy food, minced meat, puppy formula or anything else the breeder has fed with success up to that point.

## ESTABLISHING A ROUTINE

Stick to the feeding regime your puppy is used to for the first week or two. Over the next few months, though, you will be gradually increasing the amount of food he is given with each meal, and reducing the number of meals overall. As a rule of thumb, you can take the meals down to around three a day at four months, and two a day from nine months. Be guided by your puppy on this. If he seems hungry between larger meals or has an upset stomach when you're increasing the amount of food, take a step back and try again in another week or two. While it's natural for puppies to have upset stomachs every so often, if your puppy often vomits or has diarrhoea, take him to the veterinarian.

Always feed your puppy in the same spot, and have a bowl of fresh water there all the time. Clean the drinking bowl daily, at the same time that you wash his food bowl. Give him 15 minutes to eat and when he wanders away from the bowl, remove it. Most puppies will clear their plates well within the time limit, but if yours doesn't, take the food away and give fresh food at the next mealtime. It's healthier (in hot weather uneaten dog food may attract flies), and it's easier to keep track of how much your dog is eating if he is having proper meals rather than endless snacks.

## CASE HISTORY
### Solving digestive problems

Nero, an otherwise healthy eight-month-old pointer puppy, was continually being taken to the veterinarian with digestive problems. His owner, Barbara, found that any slight changes in the regime he'd had since being a small puppy led to attacks of vomiting and diarrhoea.

The veterinarian made various suggestions, including a sensitive-stomach branded formula and BARF (raw food) diet (see pages 100–101), but there wasn't much improvement in the puppy's condition. After eight weeks of experimenting the veterinarian then suggested adding a probiotic supplement to Nero's diet – a mix of bacterias and yeasts, believed to boost the immune system. Barbara was doubtful, as she was beginning to believe that Nero was only ever going to be able to tolerate his puppy diet, but she agreed to try it out.

In Nero's case, probiotics proved to be the crucial step in stabilizing his digestion. Shortly after starting on them he was able to move onto an adult diet and, a month later, adjusted to a daily two-meal regime without further problems.

## WHAT DOGS NEED TO EAT

If your puppy is a good trencherman and is clearly happy and developing well on what you give him, you could simply carry on feeding him a 'mature' version of the diet he was on when he came home with you. However, just as you should pay attention to your own diet, it's worth familiarizing yourself with the different elements that make up good canine nutrition.

Below: Broccoli and other fresh vegetables can be a valuable source of vitamins. Your pet will find them more digestible if they've been lightly cooked.

## TIPS AND ADVICE
### Basic dietary requirements

These are the building blocks of canine nutrition, which must be incorporated into your dog's diet:

- **PROTEIN.** Available in meat, fish, eggs and some dairy foods. Protein is a basic necessity for growth and development in a puppy and a key energy source for all dogs.
- **FAT.** As well as supplying energy, fat in the diet supplies fatty acids, which play a vital role in maintaining a dog's health. The most beneficial fats of all are found in oily fish and nuts and seeds. Most protein sources also contain some fat.
- **CARBOHYDRATES.** Opinions are divided as to how much carbohydrate dogs need, although most commercial pet foods contain a lot. Carbs, found in wheat, oats, barley, corn, rice and other grains, are a good source of energy. Most, depending on how processed they are, also contain a fair amount of

fibre. Dogs have a short gut and tend to process food relatively quickly, but some fibre is thought to be generally beneficial to a dog's digestion, helping to prevent constipation or diarrhoea.
- **VITAMINS AND MINERALS.** Unlike humans, dogs are able to manufacture vitamin C in their livers and don't usually need to take any extra (although some practitioners recommend supplements in breeds that are susceptible to arthritis). They do need plenty of vitamins A, B group, D, E and K, plus a balance of minerals including calcium, sulphur and magnesium. If a dog has a good and balanced diet, he shouldn't need supplements, although a veterinarian may sometimes suggest one or more to help combat a specific problem.

## KEEPING THINGS CALM

Resource-guarding at mealtimes can be a problem with adult dogs, as it's natural for them to be possessive around their food. While you should let your dog eat in peace, it's a nuisance if the guarding goes over the top. To eliminate the problem, you can discourage him from doing this while he is still a puppy.

When you feed him, start by putting only half the food into your puppy's bowl. Take the bowl away just before he finishes the last mouthful, add the rest of the food and give the bowl back to him. This is easy to do while your dog is still small, and if you do it regularly and consistently (which means often, not necessarily at every single meal) it will give him good associations around having his food bowl taken away. Once the association that bowl removed equals more food, is clear in your dog's head, you can refresh the memory occasionally with food handouts mid-meal.

Below: **Kibble or dried dog food is available in every imaginable flavour and formula, from puppy mix to recipes for diabetic dogs.**

## CHECKLIST
## Don't feed!

There are many foods that humans eat that dogs shouldn't. A few are actually dangerous for dogs, and even more so for puppies. Never leave any of the following anywhere that a curious puppy might find it.

- **CHOCOLATE** contains theobromine, a substance that dogs can't digest and which can have an adverse effect on the nervous system.
- **GRAPES AND RAISINS.** No one knows why, but both grapes and raisins can be poisonous to dogs. Even a dog that has eaten them without problems can become ill when eating them again.
- **ONIONS AND GARLIC** contain substances called sulfoxides and disulfides. These can damage the red blood cells and are implicated in a disease called hemolyitic anaemia, which affects the immune system and can be fatal. Garlic is an ingredient in some dog treats, but is used only in extremely small (and thus safe) quantities.
- **ALCOHOL.** Dogs are susceptible to the effects of alcohol and have no resistance to it. Alcoholic poisoning can be fatal.

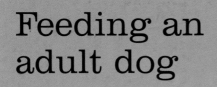

# Feeding an adult dog

If you got your dog as a puppy you'll be working out his diet as he grows and finding out what does and doesn't suit him. With an adult dog, you're taking on an unknown palate, perhaps without knowing much about what the dog has been fed before.

Try to find out as much as possible: ask the shelter or society he comes from what he's been eating with them when you collect him and, just as you would with a puppy, keep him on the same diet for a week or two while he's getting used to his new surroundings, even if you plan to change it eventually.

## IS HE THE RIGHT WEIGHT?
Use the first visit to the veterinarian to ask about your dog's condition. Is he too fat or too thin? In what kind of condition are his skin and coat? Ask the veterinarian if there are any particular foods or supplements that your dog would benefit from.

If you have a breed dog, you can check with the kennel club statistics to see if he falls within weight guidelines for the breed. If your dog is a mongrel, there are a couple of simple tests you can do to see if he is more or less the right weight. When you handle him, can you feel his ribs individually without much prodding or poking? If you run your hand down his spine, can you feel his

backbone? And seen sideways, in silhouette, is there a visible 'tuck' between your dog's back legs and the point at which his ribcage ends – a concave curve where the stomach tucks up towards the back of the body? If the answers to these three questions are yes, no, yes, your dog is neither too fat nor too thin. If, on the other hand, you can't really feel his ribs and rather than a tuck he has a solid, saggy stomach, he's probably overweight. And if you can feel the knobs of his spine in his back, it's likely that he is too thin.

These are simple rules of thumb and may not apply to every breed. Greyhounds, lurchers and whippets, for example, are thinner than many other breeds, while bulldogs or some of the larger mastiff breeds are naturally deep-chested and may appear stocky without being overweight. Others, such as the Labrador, have a tendency to gain weight, which calls for vigilance by their owners. Smaller dogs usually need slightly more food in ratio to their weight than larger ones.

Above: **Older dogs can suffer from health problems if they're not kept at a healthy weight.**

## FEEDING OPTIONS

There are numerous feeding options for today's pet dog. The one you eventually fix on will depend on how much you can afford to pay, what you decide is the best bet nutritionally, how much time you can dedicate to feeding your dog (some options call for home-cooked meals) and – ultimately – what suits him best.

There are two main categories of commercial dog food: dried or tinned. Both are sold as 'complete' foods, meaning they give the dog everything he needs in terms of nutrients. Both are available in a range of prices, from economical to rather more costly. The fact that they are marketed as 'complete' foods doesn't, of course, prevent you from either augmenting them, or from feeding your dog a mix of commercial food and fresh or home-cooked food.

Dried food is cheaper (even if you pick one of the more expensive brands) and it easier to store. Tinned food contains more water, which is useful if your dog isn't a big drinker, and may be more acceptable to fussy eaters, who won't always eat dry food. One of the less palatable aspects of dried food is its creation by a compression process at a very high temperature, which removes much of its vitamin value. To ensure that the food still has the recommended nutritional values, after 'cooking' the kibble is sprayed with a mix of flavouring, vitamins and oil, which also increases its palatability to dogs.

Most dogs are fed manufacturer's dog food and plenty of dogs thrive on it. If you decide to feed your dog a diet of commercial food, research the best-quality brands. Dog food labelling can be hard to interpret and the rules about the content of dog food are very different from those applied to the foods people eat. You're looking in particular for mention of 'meat' or 'chicken' or 'poultry' rather than qualified expressions such as 'rendered meat products' or 'meat meal'. In the same way, 'whole grains' is better than 'grain products', 'grain meal' or similar.

If you're doubtful, ask your veterinarian to recommend a high-quality brand that doesn't contain any of the less palatable by-products of the food industry.

## HOME-COOKED FOOD

If you don't want to give your dog commercially produced food, you can opt for a home-cooked diet. You can make this as simple or as varied as suits your schedule (and your dog). While some fans will cook up different recipes every few days, others stick to a few tried and tested meals that they know their dogs like and which seem to suit them.

Home-cooked meals may be a mixture of raw and cooked food. They combine protein, carbohydrates and often some extras such as brewer's yeast or a little fish oil. If you're dealing with a dog who has a sensitive digestion, take advice from your veterinarian before putting him on a home-cooked diet, and ask for recipe sheets or, if your veterinarian doesn't supply these, some guidance on the relative quantities of different sorts of food. A typical home-cooked meal might, for example, contain some cooked oats and chicken with vegetables and perhaps a little oily fish, simmered together, cooled and served with the cooking water.

Some owners opt to feed a mix of home-cooked and commercial. An example would be dry kibble with some chopped raw beef or cooked chicken, and perhaps a small amount of cooked vegetables, such as broccoli or carrot.

## THE RAW FOOD DIET

The BARF diet (that is, the Biologically Appropriate Raw Food diet – or, as it is more often known, the Bones And Raw Food diet) has many fans, and some owners who feed their dogs BARF believe that it is the only true natural diet for a dog. BARF is based on the idea that, in the wild, dogs would eat whole animals, including bones, organs, fur and feathers, and that this is still the biologically appropriate diet for them.

In the debate on whether dogs are omnivores or carnivores, BARF adherents come down firmly on the carnivore side, arguing that dogs would never naturally eat carbohydrate and processed grains and that it's damaging for their diet to contain them. The typical BARF diet will consist largely of raw meat, some on the bone, with additional smaller quantities of some vegetables and dairy foods.

Left: **Dogs can manufacture their own vitamin C within their bodies, but they need a regular supply of other vitamins and minerals, such as vitamin A from carrots.**

Left: **Many owners opt for a mix of commercial and home-cooked foods for their pet. This gives a dog some home-cooked favourites, plenty of nutrients and the high water content from tinned food, plus the option of dry foods for the fussy eater.**

Opinions are divided as to how healthy the diet is. Certainly it has digestive and dental advantages. The amount of gnawing and chewing called for in eating large pieces of meat and raw bones keeps dogs' teeth clean and seems to be effective in solving digestive problems in some cases. Dogs enjoy the chewing and can engage with their meals in a way that isn't possible with easy-to-swallow processed food.

Critics worry about the bacteria and parasites that can be found in raw meat, particularly that not cleared for human consumption. While processed foods may contain fewer nutrients, the same processes get rid of some undesirables too. The no-camp believe that the immune systems of domestic dogs aren't as tough as those of animals living in the wild, and that dogs fed this way may therefore be more susceptible to infections as a result of their diet.

There is information available on BARF diets both in books and online. Ask your veterinarian for a balanced opinion if you are interested in feeding your dog in this way. If your dog's diet seems fine as it is and you don't want to change to something as uncompromising as BARF, at least consider giving him a large, raw beef bone every now and then. There's no doubt that most dogs really enjoy these, that they give the complex muscles of dogs' jaws and cheeks a good workout, and that they keep their teeth free of plaque.

If you decide to make changes, always make them gradually across a week or two.

## WEIGHT CONTROL

The good news about feeding a dog is that because you're in sole charge of his diet, it's usually easy to get him to drop or gain a few pounds. The rules are the same as the ones you'd apply to yourself, but there isn't the same need for willpower: you simply give your dog a little less or more food. If he needs to shed weight, an extra 30-minute walk per day or a few more games of fetch will help too.

# Grooming and bathing

The kind of coat your dog has – and therefore the amount of grooming and coat care that he needs – is not likely to have been high on your list of deciding factors when you chose him, unless you suffer from an allergy to dog hair.

Coat care can be time-consuming and you need to be prepared to do it properly, with grooming tools and a bathing routine.

## WHAT TYPE OF COAT?

Apart from its colour, a dog's coat is defined by three qualities: whether it is single or double; its length; and its texture. Dogs have either a single coat, which has consistent texture and hair thickness, or a double one, made up of a silky undercoat and a harsher layer called the topcoat. The second quality – length – is defined as short, medium or long. Short hair needs no explanation; long usually means a hair length of over 7.5 centimetres (3 in); medium, as you'd expect, comes somewhere in between, at around 2.5–5 centimetres (1–2 in). The third quality, texture, refers to the 'finish' of a dog's coat. Dogs may have a curly finish (like the poodle), a silky finish (such as the Yorkshire terrier), or a coarse or wiry one (such as the elkhound and the Norfolk terrier respectively).

It's the combination of traits that makes a dog's coat easy or time-consuming to look after, and that decides whether he's a heavy, constant shedder of hair or instead enjoys regular seasonal moults. The least demanding dogs in grooming terms are small breeds with short, single coats. This doesn't mean that these breeds won't be heavy shedders, simply that they are easy to groom. The most challenging combination of all is a large dog with a heavy double coat that also moults heavily (such as, for example, the Newfoundland). A handful of breeds

Left: The tiny bent wires in the head of a slicker grooming brush pull all the loose hair out of the coat.

such as the poodle or the Portuguese Water dog hardly shed at all, but these dogs' curly coats need very regular grooming.

## A GROOMING ROUTINE

If you have a puppy, whatever his coat type, buy a soft brush and comb and get him used to short grooming sessions. Begin by brushing him gently all over, starting on the back and flanks, the areas he is least likely to fuss about, and progressing to head, chest, paws and belly. When you've been over him with the brush, go over once again with the comb. Check his ears and between his toes.

If you're dealing with an adult dog who is unused to being groomed, set about things gently. He can stand on a table or on a sheet on the floor while you work around him. Have plenty of treats to hand, start on the least sensitive areas and deal gently with the parts of the body that most dogs don't like being touched, such as the paws. Hold your dog firmly but not roughly. Most dogs come to enjoy grooming. If you have a large dog who isn't completely compliant, enlist a helper to hold him and keep him happy while you groom.

Make sure that you brush and comb right down to the skin. The topcoat is comparatively easy to comb out, so start underneath and work up to the top, combing through any mats. If your dog is groomed regularly you shouldn't have to cope with many dense knots, but make sure you get right around your dog in every session – a neglected undercoat may require professional help.

## CHECKLIST
## Grooming equipment

You'll need some or all of the following for your grooming routine:

**STEEL COMB.** This should have graduated teeth, finer at one end than the other. It's useful for all coat types. Choose a comb appropriate to the size of dog.

**SLICKER BRUSH.** A brush with a rectangular head that is densely filled with fine, short wires. This is useful for pulling out loose hairs from most breeds and redundant undercoat. Again, choose an appropriate size.

**GROOMING RAKE.** Shaped as it sounds, with widely spaced long teeth, this literally drags out the deep layer of redundant undercoat in large, densely double-coated dogs.

**SOFT BRUSH OR GROOMING MITT.** This 'polishes' short-coated dogs after brushing. The grooming mitt has a rubber palm with a nubbed texture that is used in a massaging stroke.

**GROOMING SHEET.** You can buy a grooming sheet at the pet shop, or simply use an old sheet to confine the shedding. It's useful for small dogs and essential for big ones.

## BATHING AT HOME

If you have a very large breed you may prefer your dog to be bathed at the groomer's. Most dogs can be bathed at home provided that you prepare in advance and have everything to hand when you need it.

Small dogs can be bathed in the sink and larger breeds in the bath itself. Brush and comb your dog before his bath, as bathing can make existing mats in a dog's coat worse.

Choose a dog shampoo as human shampoos may contain ingredients that aren't good for a dog's skin. If your dog suffers from allergies (and particularly if frequent bathing has been recommended) ask your veterinarian to suggest a shampoo that will soothe rather than irritate the condition.

You'll need a handheld spray attachment that fits either the bath or sink, two plastic jugs (one filled with shampoo solution, ready diluted with hand-hot water) and several towels. Have a towel or a rubber mat for your dog to stand on; most will be frightened by slippery porcelain or plastic under their feet. Before putting your dog in the sink or bathtub, fill it with hand-hot water to a depth that will come about a third of the way up his legs.

When everything is ready, lift the dog into the sink or bath, positioning him so that he is standing on the mat, and use a plastic jug to gently pour water all over him, avoiding his eyes. When he is wet all over, pour small amounts of the shampoo solution onto his coat, starting from the head and working your way along to the tail. Work the shampoo into a lather all over the dog before rinsing. When you're ready to rinse, take the plug out and let the soapy water drain, check that the temperature of the water from the showerhead is set at lukewarm and rinse your dog thoroughly, making sure you get all the shampoo out.

Squeeze as much water out of your dog's coat as you can with your hands, then drape a towel over him and lift him onto another towel you've laid ready on the floor. Towel dry him, rubbing gently but thoroughly. Don't allow him to escape and shake himself off until he's at least halfway dry!

Left: **If your dog is unsure about his bath, a non-slip mat or towel under his feet will feel more secure.**

You can let him finish drying by a radiator, provided it's warm in your house generally, or you can finish off the process with a hair dryer and a soft brush. If you have a double-coated dog be sure to dry the underlayer as well as the topcoat.

## PROFESSIONAL GROOMING

Of course, you can opt to take your dog to be groomed by a professional. The traditional clips some dogs wear aren't possible to achieve at home, and if you have a large breed with a demanding coat you may choose to let the professionals deal with it at least some of the time. Some double-coated dogs need to be professionally stripped – a process in which the hair is removed at least partly by hand.

Find a groomer by word of mouth or recommendation, and if you haven't seen examples of their work,

Above: **Professional groomers can give your dog any cut you ask for, from a utility crop to a full show presentation – but at a cost.**

don't hesitate to ask to see a dog or dogs they've groomed. Be clear about what you are asking and what you will get.

If you want your natural standard poodle to be given a bath and a slight trim, for example, make sure the groomer understands that you're not asking for the considerably fancier look of a show clip.

If you're asking for a longer coated breed to be given a short utility cut for the summer, be certain that you understand what that will look like, and specify how long you want the hair to be, on both the head and body of your dog.

Lastly, be warned, professional grooming can be expensive.

# While you are away

At some point you will probably need your dog to be cared for by someone else – perhaps while you're away on holiday, as the result of an emergency, or just because your day-to-day life is too busy in other areas just then to give him all that he needs.

If you make the effort to find him the right carer, these times can actually enhance your dog's routine and broaden his social life.

## DOG WALKERS AND DOGGY DAYCARE

Both these services have become far more popular over the last 20 years. Dog walkers can ensure that your dog gets some exercise while you're out at work, while doggy daycare is a sort of day nursery for dogs where you can leave your pet during the day and collect him in the evening on the way home.

Both services usually require your dog to mix happily with other dogs, although there are dog-walking services that are prepared to take your dog out on his own for a slightly higher fee. The usual arrangement is that the dog walker collects your dog from your house at a pre-arranged time and takes him out for an hour or two's exercise in a group of dogs – perhaps five or six – usually to a park or, if the service is based in the countryside, to a more rural spot where your dog can have off-leash fun.

The chance to run and play with several other dogs will be much appreciated by a gregarious, dog-focused dog. It's less suitable for a more nervous type as he may not react well to finding himself as part of a large group. Some dog walkers

Below: Dog walkers usually offer a range of services, from basic walking to taking your dog out jogging.

offer 'introduction' opportunities that allow you to go for a walk with them and the dogs they look after to see if your dog will integrate happily.

Doggy daycare arrangements vary. In city locations they may have indoor play areas for the dogs, or fenced yards. In suburban or out-of-town centres, dogs may get to play together in large grassy areas. Just as with dog walking, an easy-going, dog-focused dog may love the opportunity to mix with lots of other dogs, while a dog playground may be a shy, nervous dog's worst nightmare.

Daycare in particular is not really suitable for puppies even if you find a daycare facility that takes them. The group often comprises a huge mix of dogs of all temperaments and the socializing won't be monitored as closely as you would yourself. Rather than improving your puppy's social skills, the experience is more likely to overwhelm him.

If you decide to use either a dog walker or daycare for your dog check out the service carefully. Ask for references or choose a service that's worked out for a fellow dog owner you trust. You can ask to spend an hour at a daycare facility if you're not sure – if they aren't happy for you to observe then it's probably not the right place for you or your dog.

## BOARDING KENNELS AND HOUSE SITTERS

If you need somewhere for your dog to stay for a block of time while you're on holiday, then the two main options are boarding kennels or a house sitter. While many boarding

Above: **If you hire a house sitter your dog will be able to stick to his normal walks and routine.**

kennels are carefully run and the dogs well cared for, some owners feel that they are rather bleak places – with individual wire-fronted runs, they tend to look like dog shelters. And most of the dogs in kennels are necessarily kept confined for a large part of the day. If you use a kennel, word-of-mouth recommendation, a visit and plenty of questions are the best ways of ensuring that you're leaving your pet somewhere where he will be properly looked after.

A house sitter can be someone who looks after pets and properties for a living or a friend who agrees to take care of things while you're away.

Take up references if you use the former, and ensure the arrangement is clearly defined if the latter, so that your sitter is clear how often and where you expect them to exercise your dog and whether they need to keep your dog company and play with him. Provide full details of what he eats and what you propose to pay.

# Travelling with a dog

You'll probably stay around the house for your dog's first day or two, and possibly much longer if you have a new puppy. However, sooner or later you'll want to get out and about with your dog. It will be that much easier if he's a calm traveller.

## TRAVELLING BY CAR

If you made the journey from the breeder or the shelter by car it may have been the first time that your pet had been in a vehicle. While carsickness is commonest in puppies, it can also affect adult dogs that haven't travelled in a car much.

Most dogs get over it as they have more frequent car trips, but to avoid your dog developing a long-term dislike keep your journeys with him short at first. Furthermore, make sure you're headed to a destination that he likes, such as the park or out for a walk in nearby countryside.

Avoid car journeys straight after your pet's mealtime, open the windows enough to keep fresh air circulating in the car and see if a different position in the car (sitting in the front rather than the back seat, for example) reduces his sickness, if it's a problem. You should secure the dog in the car while you're driving, either by fitting him with a safety harness, which fits into the seatbelt mechanism, or by shutting him in his crate on longer journeys.

Below: **To the great majority of dogs, a trip in the car – particularly en route to a walk – is a valued treat.**

Crates can actually make a dog feel safer in transit and sometimes alleviate carsickness. If you opt not to secure your dog (and plenty of drivers don't, despite recommendations) at least make sure he sits in the back seat. If you're in even a minor accident, the inflation of an air bag in the front could seriously hurt him.

Even if it makes them uneasy at first, most dogs come to love car travel, with the opportunities it offers to see the world passing by and – often – a walk or a visit as a payoff. Some especially love sticking their heads right out of the car windows. Even if your dog enjoys this, it can cause inflammation of the eyes, and most veterinarians advise against it.

## WHEN YOU ARRIVE

If your dog is shut in a crate or held in a harness, you won't need to worry about him leaping out of the car when you reach your destination. But if you opt to have your dog loose in the car, or if he even occasionally travels without a crate or harness, make sure he becomes accustomed to waiting for a word from you before he gets out. It may be fine for him to leap out when you've reached the beach or are going for a rural walk, but it isn't safe if you've parked on a busy city street, and your dog won't understand the difference.

## OTHER FORMS OF TRANSPORT

Don't take a puppy on the bus or train until he has completed his first course of shots. When you do take your dog on public transport, be considerate to other passengers.

Above: **Your dog does need to be under control at all times if you travel on public transport together.**

Don't assume that everyone at close quarters will welcome making your dog's acquaintance, and try to travel at a time of day when you won't be in a crowd. If your dog tends to get nervous or over-excited, make sure you keep him near you. A short leash and a harness, rather than a collar, are the best ways to make sure that he remains under your control.

## WARNING

Dogs should never be left in the car for long periods, and they shouldn't be left there at all in warm weather. Cars can become as hot as ovens very quickly on a fine day, and even if you park in the shade and leave windows open, it will get far too hot for your dog. Dogs heat up fast and can't sweat through their skin. Add a fur coat to the mix and you can end up with a dog with heatstroke or worse.

# Meeting new people

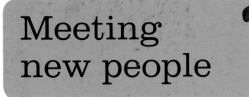

How much does your dog like people he doesn't know? You probably won't know until he meets someone he *doesn't* like. Puppies tend to greet all contacts with enthusiasm, provided that they're given no reason to find the novelty threatening.

Older dogs have mixed reactions depending on the lessons they've already learned about people. Puppy or adult, a dog is sometimes made fearful by something unfamiliar in someone new, whether it's the fact that they carry a stick, wear a hat or simply, as in the case history opposite, are wearing heavier-than-usual clothes that change their silhouette.

Left: **Teaching your dog to formally 'greet' new people may alleviate his nervousness by giving him something specific to do.**

## DEALING WITH FEARFUL RESPONSES

If a dog is acting fearful around a person, don't rebuke him. It's his prerogative to decide what he's frightened of, much as it's your job as owner to deal with the situation and to reassure him. The best short-term answer is to get him away from the source of his fear. Don't let the person he is finding frightening try to reassure him, either by bending down to his level and getting into his space or by holding out a hand and urging the dog to 'say hello!'. This could make your dog feel that he's been backed into a corner where his only option is to snap. If you're at home suggest your dog goes to his place – crate, basket or safe corner. If you're out and about, move slightly away from the person who's scaring him.

## COUNTER-CONDITIONING

If your dog seems to find specific aspects of new people intimidating, you can use classic counter-conditioning. This means that you change his responses by changing the associations he has with the thing he fears. Usually it calls on you to enlist some help and to stage situations in which a person in a hat, say, or one wheeling a bike, throws him treats.

Work gradually over two or three sessions on this. The idea is that the treats are dispensed closer and closer to the subject of his fear, and that the fear fades to be replaced with anticipation of a treat. It usually works, but it takes patience as it isn't always a fast solution.

You might have a dog that isn't fearful, but boisterous and keen to be everyone's friend. Train him to sit to be introduced to someone new, and don't perform the 'introduction' until he's sitting. If he still tries to jump, get the person you're introducing to body-block your dog (see pages 122–3) so that he doesn't have the pleasure of a personal encounter until he does what you ask.

Below: **Don't push a new dog to get up close and personal with people he doesn't know. In-your-face contact is rude in dog terms.**

## CASE HISTORY
### Recognizing the unfamiliar

Rachel was the proud owner of a five-month-old collie cross. The puppy had dealt with meeting a wide range of people and other dogs with enthusiasm and a good grace. Rachel was therefore surprised when, one day, she opened the door to a friend her dog had met before and he started to growl. As Rachel's friend came into the hallway the puppy backed off and started to bark. Rather upset, Rachel suggested he go to his crate in the kitchen.

Ten minutes later, Rachel allowed the puppy into the living room, where he greeted the friend with enthusiasm as usual. Rachel dismissed the incident at the doorway as a one-off, but a week later it happened again, with the same visitor. This time the visitor paid no attention, but instead came inside and took off his outdoor clothes. As he shed his 'disguise', the dog stepped forward, wagging, as if he had just noticed someone he knew.

It's easy to see why the dog behaved as he did. He had seen an amorphous shape, loaded with hat, coat and scarf and not recognized it as a person, much less someone he knew.

# Pre-training for a puppy

Once a new puppy is on his way to being housebroken and is used to being handled, you can add a little daily pre-training to his routine. This will stand you in good stead when you start 'real' training when he's a little older.

Keep the sessions regular and try not to skip days, but make the lessons short – no longer than ten minutes – so that he doesn't get bored (puppies under 16 weeks have a short attention span), and always finish with a game.

Not only will these early lessons help to teach him a few basics, they should also encourage him to look to you for any interpretation he needs about what's going on around him. A dog that refers to you because he trusts you, will be easier to train and to socialize as his world expands.

## LEARNING HIS NAME

Although words have no intrinsic meaning for dogs, they can be invested with a wide range of meanings. We don't know whether a dog that responds to his name thinks 'that's me!' or whether he simply knows that he'll be rewarded with your attention if he turns to look at you when he hears it.

Whichever is the case, dogs are usually quick to learn to respond. The 'action' you want is a focus on you when you call him, so reward him for just looking at you. He doesn't have to come – although it's fine if he does – but start by saying his name calmly and quietly when you're standing right by him, and treat and praise him the moment he looks at you. When he looks towards you whenever he hears his name, even if he's distracted, you can gradually reduce the treating. Always use a positive, upbeat tone when you call his name.

## TEACHING RECALL

A dog that comes back to you when called, cheerfully and reliably, will have a much more enjoyable time than a pet with uncertain recall because he'll be off the leash that much more often. You can begin to teach a puppy to 'come' as soon as he's responding to his name. Call his name from a short distance away, and when he looks up, say 'come!' in the same cheerful tone, while holding up a treat. Give it to him as soon as he arrives at your side, and practise recall whenever you have a spare moment or two, sometimes as part

of a teaching session and sometimes randomly, when your puppy is doing something else. If he delays or is slow, try not to repeat the command more than once, and praise and treat him as usual whenever he obeys.

Your puppy should always have good associations with coming to you. We've all seen the contradiction of the owner who calls and calls their dog and who, when he finally does come, scolds him. That won't make for a reliable recall in the long run. If your puppy is slow, you could always try running away from him while calling, encouraging him to chase you. Few puppies can resist this.

Above: **Don't punish accidents, but clear up very thoroughly to ensure he won't repeat the mistake.**

## WEARING A COLLAR

If your puppy hasn't been wearing a collar consistently over his first week or two with you because he's been mainly around the house, by 12 weeks it's time he got used to wearing one full time. The best puppy collars are soft – fabric, nylon or leather – and close with a flat sliding closure or a buckle. You should just be able to fit two fingers between the collar and your dog's neck, which indicates that it fits closely but isn't too tight. Attach an engraved metal disk with an address, your name and number to your puppy's collar. Your puppy will probably wriggle around and try to get his collar off at first. Provided that you have checked it isn't too tight, don't worry about this, but do check every week that the collar hasn't grown too tight as he grows. Most collars can be adjusted in size, but he'll probably still get through two or three before he reaches his adult size.

## BASIC INSTINCT **Clearing up scent messages**

Even after a puppy has been housetrained, he will probably still have the occasional accident in the house. Because dogs often use previous marker scents as a stimulus to mark again, it's key that you remove any scent messages that your dog has left, so that he doesn't have a scent 'reminder' to soil the same spot again. Regular cleaning materials may not eliminate the scent sufficiently for it to be missed by a dog's sensitive nose, but you can buy patent cleaners at the supermarket or the pet shop for this specific purpose.

# Training, exercise and games

Dogs need exercise for all the same reasons that humans do. An energetic run helps to keep a dog lean, and is beneficial for him mentally as well as physically. A properly exercised dog is less likely to chew furniture, dig holes in the garden, or develop displacement activities such as constant barking. And play – with dogs or people – incorporated into his exercise schedule gives your dog the best of both worlds: a great workout along with the chance to have fun with his canine friends and deepen the bond with his human ones.

When it's approached properly, with positive reinforcement, dogs enjoy training too. Most love to learn something new and welcome the opportunity of getting praise and attention from their owners. This chapter covers the amount and type of exercise your dog needs, a whole range of games and tricks you can try, and the various sorts of training you can use to turn your pet into a model canine citizen.

# How much exercise?

How much exercise should you give your dog? For many adult dogs, the answer would be 'more than he gets now'. The majority of veterinarians' surveys report that pet dogs are under-exercised, while few suffer from exercise exhaustion.

Exercise will ensure a dog's body stays fit and youthful. What's more, research shows that the right amount of the right sort of activity can help reduce stress, keep a temperamental dog on an even keel, and prevent problem behaviours, particularly in very alert and reactive dogs that always have to be doing something. It is better to have your dog out in the park chasing a Frisbee, than at

Right: **Flat-faced dogs need to be exercised carefully to ensure they don't overheat.**

home obsessively herding the cat or running in endless circles, just two of many alternative activities that clever, energetic dogs have come up with when left too much to their own devices.

Even if you have a dog that seems content with relatively low amounts of activity, it's worth putting some effort into keeping him fit. That said, there are some exceptions to the 'exercise good, more exercise better' rule. Strenuous exercise is not always advisable for puppies or old and rheumatic dogs, for example, and not every sort of exercise suits every type of dog. For some pets, a dream exercise session would consist of running freely somewhere safe and spacious, where they can go flat out without anyone needing to recall them. For others, it would be rushing around in a group of canine friends, or playing fetch or Frisbee, or even acting as an exercise buddy for an owner who's trying to get into shape themselves. And plenty of older or less active dogs (or the brachycephalic – flat-faced – types

such as bulldogs or pugs) find regular walks, sedately conducted, suit their abilities better than full-on, energetic exercise sessions. Remember that any type of moving around counts – exercise doesn't have to mean fast and furious.

## BREED LIMITATIONS

Although the size of your dog isn't necessarily directly related to how much stamina he has (some types of small dogs, particularly those in the terrier group, seem tireless, while some of the larger or giant breeds don't have as much energy as you might expect), there are other factors that will affect his exercise needs. The requirements of very small dogs – many of the toy group, for example – should be considered relatively: 1.75 kilometres (2 miles) may be a stroll

for a young Labrador or golden retriever, but it's a long walk for a Chihuahua. Brachycephalic dogs, as mentioned above, are particularly susceptible to overheating and it's not sensible to over-exercise them, or sometimes, if the weather's very warm, to exercise them at all. Some of the heavily-coated large breeds too (such as Newfoundlands or St Bernards), don't do well in high temperatures. This is doubly true for puppies or elderly dogs in these categories. Regardless of breed, in hot weather it's always sensible to give your dog his walks and play sessions in the early morning or evening, when it is cooler.

## CASE HISTORY
### The right kind of exercise

Sarah found her eight-month-old pet at a breed rescue society. Casey was a miniature dachshund – so petite that he looked like a stuffed toy. When Sarah got him home, however, he proved to be strong minded and determined, and fixed on energetic play. When he was out with other dogs, he was the first to leap after a ball or Frisbee.

Sarah worried, because she'd been warned about dachshunds' propensity for back strain. But she hated to spoil Casey's fun. She called the rescue society secretary, who suggested channelling Casey's energies into training. Sarah was doubtful, but enrolled Casey in a beginners' agility class. From the start it was a success. Casey learned fast, and was given a special course tailored to dogs with vulnerable backs, that included weave poles, tunnels and seesaw exercises rather than jumps. He loved the classes so much that Sarah set up a miniature course for him in her garden and gives him practice every day. In his eagerness to practise agility, Casey seems to have forgotten about Frisbees altogether.

## PUPPY EXERCISE

How much, how soon? There's a lot of confusion around whether or not it's safe for a puppy to have strenuous exercise. Some breeders and veterinarians issue warnings against long walks with any dog under a year old, while others say that a puppy over six months can be exercised until evidently physically tired. If your puppy is pedigree-bred, ask about his exercise requirements when you collect him, as his breeder will be the expert on what's best. If you have a young mixed-breed dog, use your common sense and, when he's finished his first course of vaccinations, build up to longer

Below: **Most dogs enjoy sniffing around the backyard. Outdoor time doesn't equate to 'exercise', however, unless your dog is actively walking or playing.**

walks gradually – assume that when his enthusiasm starts to flag, it's time to head home. If you're going to be out for more than an hour or so, even if you won't be actively exercising all the time, always remember to take along a portable water bottle and bowl for your dog and offer water regularly. Dogs can become dehydrated without very much warning, and it's a condition that can be dangerous.

Right: **Puppies exercise enthusiastically but tire faster than adult dogs. Be ready to take your pet home as soon as he starts flagging.**

## CHECKLIST
## Good puppy practice

### Do

- Allow your puppy to play outdoors in your own garden from just a few weeks old. It's good for even very small puppies to experience different smells and textures.
- Let your puppy play until he is tired, but if a puppy suddenly falls asleep, leave him to nap until he wakes up naturally. All puppies have sudden spurts of frenetic energy, interspersed by periods of rest time.
- Check for signs that your puppy is tired when he's out. The face of a tired puppy tends to look less 'full', and the relaxed, 'happy'-looking mouth may appear tighter at the corners. Learn to recognize his tired expression and take it as a sign that it's time to head home.

### Don't

- Encourage a puppy to do much jumping or leaping. Over-exertion can damage developing joints and ligaments until a dog is fully grown.
- Allow a puppy to climb endlessly up and down stairs or on and off furniture, for the same reason – it isn't good for his growing joints. Long-backed dogs such as dachshunds or Dandie Dinmont terriers should be discouraged from climbing or jumping even as adults, because the backs of these long breeds are susceptible to slipped disks and other problems.

# Different kinds of exercise

If you grew up with a pet whose exercise comprised half-hour walks on the leash, the variety of activities available to dogs today may amaze you. Many dogs are still simply walked around, but there's now less excuse for not offering more.

Left: **It's not just large breeds that enjoy agility. Most dogs will love a course tailored to suit their abilities.**

Similarly, whereas the choice of toys used to be limited to ball or stick, there's now a brightly coloured array of things that roll, squeak, ring and bounce, to appeal to all tastes.

You may want to think about local dog training classes and organizations. The many possibilities include agility classes; flyball – a jump-and-catch relay activity that's wonderful for dogs that are ball-mad; doggy dancing; obedience classes and trials; and working-dog trials, which include digging (for terriers) and field trials (for gundogs and hounds). Sledding and skijoring – in which a dog pulls a skier, often much loved by huskies and other northern breeds such as malamutes and Samoyeds – are still limited to areas that can depend on regular snowfall, but most other activities are widely available and all you need to do is turn up.

Of course, you have to have achieved a degree of basic obedience to pursue any of these options, but if you have a dog that, from the first, has shown a particular interest in and aptitude for, say, tracking a scent or hurdling a fence, he'll probably enjoy learning to use his skill in an organized environment.

## WATER PLAY
One of the most powerful draws for many dogs, particularly the retrieving breeds such as Labradors, retrievers and spaniels, is water.

If your dog loves swimming and playing in water more than anything else, you'll know how hard it is to keep him from leaping straight into any water he sees, whether it's the sea, a local lake, or a fast-flowing river. Many dogs even enjoy a dip in the family swimming pool.

Water has dangers for dogs, however. An apparently slow river or calm sea can hide currents too powerful for your pet to swim against. While generally not dangerous in the same way, if the water is stagnant, lakes may contain

Above: **Don't assume that unfamiliar waters are fine for swimming. Keep your dog leashed until you've checked with a local that the river or sea is safe.**

algae that will make a dog ill. Even swimming pools can be problematic if they don't have ramps or other means for a dog to climb out.

There are likely to be plenty of places where your dog can swim safely – and you can watch him enjoying himself – but if he's a true water enthusiast he won't pause to consider the perils before jumping in, so *you* have to be the cautious one.

If you're somewhere unfamiliar, where your dog hasn't swum before, talk to locals before allowing him off the leash. See where other dogs are swimming and take your guidance from their owners. And keep an eye on your dog around other people's swimming pools. If you have a pool yourself, get a ramp installed so that even if your dog accidentally gets in when there's no one is around, he'll be able to get out.

## WARNING

Always check that still water is clear before allowing your dog to swim. If it's thick with weed and algae or opaquely green, don't let him get in. A dog will inevitably take in some water when swimming and water in this state is not safe to drink.

# Introducing training

At some point in your puppy's life, general socialization will need to incorporate formal training. Most puppies won't have the concentration to manage training sessions successfully before 12 weeks, but it's never too early to introduce the idea.

If you do start training early, don't be discouraged if the lessons don't seem to 'take'. Simply leave it another week and then try again.

## BREAKING BAD HABITS

As well as learning new things, your puppy may need to unlearn a few bad habits. The most common of all is nipping while you're handling him or when he becomes over-excited – whether in play, or while you're trying to teach him something. Never allow any nipping without an immediate reaction. The moment he closes his teeth a bit too hard say 'Owwww' on a sharp, high note (the more you can make it sound like a yelp of pain, the better) and turn your head away from him. Don't make eye contact, and if you're holding him, put him down. Don't look at him again or re-engage with him at all for a minute or two. You may feel mean – after all, he didn't consciously intend to hurt you – but nipping is a very bad habit, and in an adult dog can be dangerous. You don't want your pet thinking that biting is OK, ever, so it's important to stop it while he's still small. You will probably have to repeat the 'owww' reaction several times, but eventually he'll get the message.

## BASIC INSTINCT **Seeking attention**

For most dogs – being hardwired to look for attention from you, their leader – any interaction with you is better than none. For this reason, disapproval that focuses on the dog may not be effective. Certainly your dog would prefer praise, but even though you're not praising him, you are at least concentrating on him. Rather than respond to him, learn to ignore unwanted behaviour, and encourage what you do want. It may not come naturally but it will put across the right message in your dog's world, so it's much more likely to be effective.

Don't forget that puppies need to chew. Ensure that a selection of permitted chewables is always available, and after time out for nipping, offer your puppy a chew bone or a hard rubber toy that he can chew as much as he wants.

## BODY BLOCKING

If your puppy or adult dog jumps up at you and you want him to stop, your natural human instinct will be to hold out your hands to fend him off. Usually (and equally instinctively) you'll be saying 'No! Get down!' loudly as you push at him. This won't work: as far as your dog's concerned. In holding your hands out ('pawing' him) you're engaging with him, and by raising your voice you may even turn the unwelcome jumping into a game.

To send the message that you want him to get down, body block your dog instead. This doesn't involve using your hands, and sends the dog an unambiguous message. Ideally you want to catch him before his paws hit your body, so you have to be quick: as the dog's paws leave the floor, turn from him at an angle and hold your leg out and up slightly, leaving him nothing for his paws to gain purchase on. As you body block, say 'No', in a low, firm tone. With nothing for his paws to rest on, your dog will fall back to the floor and you can kneel down beside him and stroke him as a reward. If he already knows how to respond to commands, you could ask him to 'sit' at this point, refocusing him on something you do want him to do, and then reward him with a treat or praise.

## LEARN HOW **Body blocking**

1 Hands up, leg out and body slightly turned away all make for an unsatisfactory 'jump up' for your dog.

2 When you've successfully blocked the jump up, you can reward your dog with attention (but only after all four feet are back on the ground!).

## TRAINING THE CHILDREN

If a dog lives with a family, he needs to learn that the children outrank him and must be treated respectfully. Equally, the children need to treat the dog with respect and not become over-excited around dogs. Children offer several challenges to a dog that adults do not. Their voices are higher in pitch, and less predictable and so is the way they move – small children often rush around, then are still for a moment, then run again. This sort of noise and movement will stimulate most dogs: the shrill pitch is exciting, as is the unpredictable movement.

Traditional behaviourist wisdom says that both provoke a dog's 'prey drive', encouraging him to chase and attack. For this reason you should never leave even a well-trusted dog unsupervised around young children, much less a growing puppy, who is more unpredictable.

It's not fair to expect a dog, and particularly a puppy, to be the one that exhibits all the self-control. You can't stop children behaving naturally, but you can and should teach them to act sensibly around all dogs from a young age.

## FOLLOW-MY-LEADER

Once a puppy is used to wearing his collar and has worn his leash loose for a few days, you can begin practising the sort of play that will eventually teach him to walk to heel. Walking to heel can take a long time to teach, because – unlike 'sit', 'down' or 'come', all things your dog does sometimes anyway – there is no natural behaviour that it resembles.

### CHECKLIST
### Etiquette for children around dogs

- If a dog is friendly, pet him gently. Don't stand directly in front of him, or pat him on the head. Instead move towards him from the side and stroke its side or chest.
- Don't ever put your face level with a dog's or stare into its eyes. The dog may think you're a threat and might bite.
- Take care with the noises you make around dogs. Don't scream or rush around near them unless you know them very well.
- Don't ever play-wrestle with a dog, even one you're familiar with, and not even if you've seen an adult do this.
- If you want to pet a dog you don't know, always ask the owner first to check that the dog is friendly. Never rush up to a strange dog.

The best way to start teaching your dog to walk with you is to turn following you into a game. This way of teaching has several stages and blurs the distinction between training and play. The advantage is that your dog thinks he's playing while you know he's learning. You can also start teaching with quite a young puppy; if at any point he has difficulty with the next stage, simply return to the previous one. Old-style training, whereby owners were told to drag their puppies until they 'learned' didn't teach the puppies anything other than that if they didn't walk, it would hurt them. It isn't a good lesson.

Instead, you can use your dog's chase impulse to get him to follow you and ultimately, with plenty of patience, he will walk with you. The leash comes last in the equation. If your dog is wearing a leash as a matter of course during the game, you can eventually take it up (loosely) and walk with him, when he's happy walking alongside you. Ultimately he will neither pull nor drag on the leash, and you won't be dependent on it to control him unless an unexpected distraction arises.

This follow-my-leader game will work with most dogs, whether you're teaching a puppy or re-training an adult. The first step is to encourage him to chase you. First get his attention, then run away from him. Call his name as you do so, and make plenty of noise to keep him 'with' you. As he catches up, give him a treat, holding it down by your leg on the side you want him – eventually – to walk on, usually your left side. Then walk briskly away, breaking into a run as your dog gets closer. When he reaches you, reward him again. Practise this daily, always treating down by the leg you want the dog to 'heel' at, and treating the whole routine as a game, until your dog is happily running after you as soon as you run away. The brisker you can keep the pace, the better.

## LEARN HOW **Walking to heel**

1 Start by moving briskly away from your dog, calling him to get his attention focused on you.

2 As he starts to move towards you, run away from him, still calling, turning the chase into a game.

3 When he catches up, give him a treat, holding it closely against your left leg, then start running again.

Left: A dog that's been carefully trained to walk on a leash has more freedom – because it's easier to take him out and about with you to all sorts of places.

that your dog moves along with you. If he gets ahead of you, change direction so that he's following you again. Don't walk up and down in an unchanging pattern as though you were on parade; instead, keep moving in different directions, changing speed and direction at whim.

The message you're trying to send to your dog is that he's walking with you, not that you're going anywhere in particular. Your ultimate aim is to get him walking alongside you whatever your pace or direction, and – eventually – whatever distractions present themselves.

The key is to ensure that the leash is always loose, so that the dog is following you rather than going his own way while tethered to you. By leaving the leash loose, you're also reducing the likelihood of your dog wanting to play tug and bite at it; he'll be more absorbed in chasing you and finding out what titbits you have for him.

## LEASH WALKING

Once your dog has learned to chase after you when you sprint away from him (and go for the treat you're holding down against your leg when he catches up with you), you can start to pick up the leash as you move away again. Keep the pace brisk, so

---

### CHECKLIST
### Good leash manners for people

- Always hold the leash on the same side – traditionally, that's your left-hand side.
- Make sure that you're alongside or ahead of your dog.
- Train little and often.

- Be enthusiastic about getting your dog to chase you – you want him to think of leash training as a game.
- Don't take your dog out and about on a leash until he's grasped the rudiments of walking with you.

As he begins to get the idea of walking with you, start to make the treating irregular. Treats should be a training aid, not an invariable lure, otherwise your dog will eventually only do what you want him to in return for the guarantee of food.

Instead give food rewards only every now and then; on other occasions, use an upbeat tone, praise and pet your dog, and treat the whole exercise as though it were an exciting game rather than a lesson that needs learning (remember, your dog doesn't know if it's a lesson or a game, only how much he's enjoying himself!).

If you ever watch dog shows or obedience classes on TV, you'll notice that the dogs featured are constantly 'checking in' with their owners, looking up at them as they walk alongside them – and, ultimately, that's how you want your dog to behave with you.

Make leash walking like this part of your training from the beginning, but practise it at different points during the day and, as with all training exercises, keep the sessions fun, short and varied. Because walking calmly and to heel on a leash is such an important element in the make-up of a well-behaved canine citizen, it's worth starting early and continuing well into adulthood.

Don't be disheartened if your new dog is older: an adult dog can be leash-trained in this way just as well as a puppy. If the adult dog has already learned to pull on a leash, it may take longer to teach him to walk alongside, but with patience and consistency, it can be done.

## LEARN HOW **Leash walking**

1 When your dog is used to chasing you and being rewarded when he catches you, pick up his leash...

2 ... and start running again. Used to the chasing game, he will happily run alongside you.

3 Reduce the run to a brisk walk, but keep changing pace and direction to keep your dog's attention on you.

# Training an older dog

If you've acquired an older dog, you will have been given some idea of the training he has received by whoever was looking after him previously. Many owners are pleased to find that their rescue dog already has good 'at home' manners.

However, over the first few weeks of ownership, it is usual that a few problem areas will emerge that require some work.

## FINDING OUT ABOUT YOUR DOG

Kennel assessments will tell you a certain amount – about whether a dog is generally confident or fearful, for example, or whether he usually gets along with other dogs. You will probably be told if your dog gets along with children too. But you won't know the detailed ins and outs of how he's going to react to your specific situation until you get him home. Even then, most adoptive dog owners discover that they have a two- or three-week 'honeymoon period' before their pet's all-round behaviour patterns start to emerge.

Below: **Give your new dog the chance to socialize both on and off the leash to give you an idea of how he gets along with other dogs.**

Right: **Try a new dog out with a variety of toys: a dog that isn't interested in playing with a ball may love a Frisbee, while others only like toys that squeak or make a noise.**

Many, many adult dogs settle in easily with very few hiccups. But even the easiest dog will benefit from a refresher course of basic training from you. If your dog knows his paces, it will help his confidence, and if he needs to learn or re-learn a few aspects of good canine citizenship, some entertaining sessions of mixed learning and play will help him to bond with you. Don't make a strong differentiation between training and playing – you can do a little leash-training, as described on the previous pages, interspersed with ball throwing or playing hide and seek, every day without your dog even noticing that he's 'being trained'. Mixing things up will keep him enthusiastic about training and encourage him to look to you for the next thing on the agenda.

Patience and consistency are just as important with an adult dog as they are with a puppy – in fact, if he comes from a less-than-ideal background in which he wasn't much thought about, or even one where he was abused, it's even more crucial. Before you think about 'testing' how well behaved he is, find out what his enthusiasms are. Is he motivated most by treats, or a ball? Is he a stick fanatic, or does he love toys that squeak? Whatever his particular triggers, once you've learned them, you know what the ultimate payoff for your dog needs to be.

## FIRST STEPS

However much variety you have in your life, this initial period isn't for introducing the unpredictable. Until you know how he reacts in lots of different circumstances, try to ensure that you're in control of situations in which you're introducing your new dog to something for the first time.

Experiment first at home. Try getting your dog to come from another part of the house when he's called. Get him to sit and lie down (if he doesn't appear to know what you're asking, move straight to pages 132–3!) If he manages to obey those commands, try 'stay'. Play with a few toys. When he's engaged with one, ask him to give it to you. If he obeys immediately, give it straight back to him – if not, try a swap with a treat or another toy – then give the first toy back to him anyway.

Above: **Let your dog start to feel confident with one or two other friendly dogs when you first take him out, before introducing him to larger groups.**

## WARNING SIGNS

**Seek professional help if your dog:**

- 'Plays' in an overbearing or aggressive way with other dogs.
- Lunges or barks with other dogs when on the leash.
- Is overly possessive with his resources – for example, growls if anyone passes him while he's playing with a toy.
- Cowers or is otherwise overtly fearful with strangers or unknown dogs.
- Has bitten – or come close to biting – for any reason whatsoever.

When you know what his parameters are at home, experiment when you're out. Try a play date with a dog you know is friendly and easygoing; take him out on the leash in different surroundings, test his recall when there are distractions (for example, a group of dogs playing in the distance). Observe carefully what he does in different situations and don't try new tests until he's passed the previous ones – don't try introducing him to several dogs all at once, for example, until he's already had friendly encounters with first just one dog, and then with two.

While you're still getting to know your dog, concentrate on spotting potential problems. When you know what, if any, concerns about his behaviour or training there are, then you can decide what to do about them.

## SOLVING PROBLEMS

The key to solving emerging problems is to deal with them effectively and quickly. Don't ever wait, worry, but do nothing until a problem behaviour has turned into an emergency. If your dog seems fearful, or is aggressive to other dogs when he's on the leash, or won't allow himself to be handled, it's better to seek professional help immediately than to hope it will work out and risk the possibility of things moving outside your control altogether and a behavioural problem turning into a crisis.

It is often more effective to take a dog that is having difficulties – of any kind – to a one-to-one session with a specialist than to rely on general training classes to put the problem right. Obedience classes are for dogs that don't have specific behaviour problems; trainers in general classes don't have much time to give each dog individually, and the mere presence of a large group of dogs in one room may over-stimulate a dog who already has impulse-control issues to the point at which a general class may be useless, or may even make things worse.

To find someone to help with behaviour issues, ask the dog owners you know, or ask your veterinarian for a referral. Word of mouth is the best recommendation. Ask about methods before you commit, and avoid anyone who uses heavy-handed 'correction' or insists that an owner should 'dominate' a dog. A trainer who stresses positive reinforcement is always the better choice.

CASE HISTORY
## Breaking bad habits

Simon bonded with his rescue dog, Buster, a three-year-old boxer, within days. Buster was quiet at home and fine with other dogs when he was playing off his leash. When he was on the leash, however, it was a different story: he lunged and barked every time he passed another dog. It wasn't any better at obedience class – as soon as he was on the leash, he began barking hysterically. Simon was concerned enough to make an appointment with a behaviourist.

- - - - - - - - - - - - - - - - - - - - - - - -

The behaviourist joined Simon and Buster on a walk so that she could observe Buster in full-on mode. Her conclusion was that Buster was over-stimulated by the presence of other dogs when he wasn't free to interact with them, and that the behaviour was the result of frustration. She suggested various ways in which Simon could bring back Buster's attention when he became over-excited, such as spraying him with water and making loud, unexpected noises. Once Simon had Buster's attention, he was able to encourage him to behave in the ways he wanted. It wasn't long before they could pass other dogs without incident.

# Perfecting the basics

If you have a puppy, you'll be teaching 'sit', 'down', 'stay' and 'come' from scratch. An adult dog, depending on his background, may need a refresher course, or you may need to begin at the beginning, just as you would with a puppy.

Whatever the situation, these four commands are the basics: the building blocks of everything your dog may learn later. You'll be using them so often that your dog should ultimately do them straight off without either of you thinking about it. So it's best to start right.

The following training exercises should be practised as part of your dog's daily routine. When he's

mastered them, you've automatically increased the number of places you can take him to visit, because his behaviour will be both controllable and reliable. Any young dog who can manage all four commands most of the time – and that includes when he's distracted by something interesting outdoors, not just when he's home alone with you – is doing very well.

## LEARN HOW 'Sit' and 'down'

1 Give the command to 'sit'. Hold the treat up and slightly back so that your dog tilts his head towards it...

2 ... and his rump starts to go down. Give him the treat at the instant his bottom hits the floor.

## BASIC INSTINCT **Trick or treat?**

What is your pet's view of treating? He probably knows a treat's a possibility when he does what you ask, but if you've alternated food treats with other things that he enjoys, then appropriate behaviour will be linked in his mind with something generally good rather than a specific reward. You don't want him to sit or stay only if you have food, in which case the treat becomes a lure, rather than a reward. In this regard, his thinking isn't unlike yours: a treat should be a possibility, rather than an inevitable payoff – what he's really enjoying the most is the interaction with you, in exactly the same way that you're taking pleasure from the interraction with him.

### DOWN

Once your dog has learned 'sit', 'down' is usually straightforward, although it may take a little longer. Have a treat in your hand but don't show it to him until you've first asked him to sit and he's already sitting. Then kneel down beside him (ask him to 'sit' again if he gets up while you're kneeling) and bring your hand, with the treat in it, down from the level of his nose to the ground, then slide your hand forward in front of him. Some dogs will lie down straight away to get the treat, others will stand up and push their nose to your hand.

Don't give the treat until your dog is lying down – if your dog simply doesn't seem to be getting the message, you can press lightly down on his upper back to suggest that he lie, but leave the choice to him and don't force him into position.

3 To teach 'down', put your dog in a sit, and slide a treat in front of his nose, saying 'down'.

4 As soon as he slides into the lying position, give him the treat. Wait until he's fully 'down' though, and don't let him nose the treat from under your hand.

Although 'down' takes longer than 'sit', most dogs will get it within a few sessions. Remember to surrender the treat the instant he starts to lie so that he can begin to make the link between the behaviour and the reward.

## STAY

While a young, active dog may find long periods of 'stay' difficult, it's quite easy to teach a brief stay to most dogs. Once he's got the idea, you can increase the length of time you ask him to stay. Help him at the start by teaching him inside, without distractions. Ensure that your dog has completely mastered 'down' before you try 'stay'; he'll get hopelessly confused if you try to teach them both at once.

First, put your dog into a 'down' in front of you. Once he's in the lying position, back up a step, hold one hand up towards your dog, palm first. Keep the palm flat and upright; you don't want him to confuse this with the hand movement he associates with 'sit'. Now say 'Stay'. Use a low, calm voice. The first few times he may leap to his feet and come towards you (although the raised, flat hand is a good visual signal he may not get it straight away). If this happens, be patient – ask him to lie down again and repeat the exercise.

The moment he gets it and stays for even a second, move back towards him and give him a treat. Act fast, so that he associates the treat with the 'stay', and not the moment that he got back up again.

## LEARN HOW 'Stay'

**1** Put your dog into a sit. Hold up your palm towards him and say 'Stay'.

**2** Take a couple of steps back, still holding your palm up. If your dog starts to get up, say 'Staaay' on a long note. As soon as he's staying for even a second, give him a treat.

3 When he can 'stay' for a second or two, alternate treats with praise. To finish his stay, say 'OK!' and open your hands to let him know it's fine to move around again.

This may take quite a few tries to get right. Until your dog can manage to stay for a few seconds in a calm and quiet environment, don't try a 'stay' anywhere that there are distractions. If you practise daily, most dogs will gradually learn to 'stay' even when they are some distance away from you and there are interesting things happening around them. Increase the difficulty of the 'stays' you ask of him slowly, one step at a time, and think of progress in terms of months, not weeks.

## COME

'Come!' should be one of the very first words in your dog's vocabulary. Like leash training, it's best practised as an integral part of his daily routine. Start by calling the word in an upbeat voice when he's coming to you anyway – and reward him as soon as he gets there. Once he's got the idea, call him to you when he's near but not yet moving towards you. Then gradually increase the distance from which you call him. When he comes every time, start to call him when he's distracted or engaged with something else.

Never fall into the common trap of scolding your dog when he eventually returns after you've called him fruitlessly for a while. Returning to you is the right thing to do, so he's earned a reward. Ignore the failures and reward the successes and he'll eventually come every time you call.

# Clicker training

Clicker training has grown immensely in popularity over the last 15 years, to the point at which most obedience or training classes will at least offer it as an option, and many use it as their sole method.

## HOW IT WORKS

In the 1940s some research into animal behaviour began to focus on operant conditioning: the idea that a repeated positive or negative outcome will eventually affect the behaviour that leads to it, so that the experience of a positive outcome makes a desired behaviour more likely. The training method that arose out of it – which was first successful with dolphins, using whistles – gradually developed into the clicker training that is used

*Below: Once he's trained, the 'click' sound will instantly get your dog's attention.*

with all sorts of animals, not just dogs, today. The clicker is a small rectangular box, usually made of plastic, with a metal tongue inside. When you press down on the tongue it emits a clear, distinctive double-click sound. The basic idea behind the training is that when your dog hears the click, he knows he's going to get a treat – and that by using the sound when he does something you want him to, you can teach him to link the behaviour to the click.

You may ask how this specific sound differs from a noise (a word or click or whistle) you could make yourself. The important difference is that, with practice, you can use the clicker to click at at the precise moment the desired behaviour happens. It's much harder to do this with a spoken instruction than you might think. The other advantage is that the clicker always makes an identical sound, unlike the human voice. Devotees believe that, provided you stick to a few very basic rules, clicker training always works. Even trainers who aren't wedded to it as a technique often use it to teach complicated tricks because it can signal the desired behaviour to the dog with such split-second timing.

## HOW YOU TRAIN

If you want to try out clicker training, the first step is to ensure that your dog makes the key association between the click sound and the treat. Arm yourself with some small treats that your dog really likes, so that you're guaranteed to get his attention. You're going to be handing a lot of them out at first, so keep them small – tiny bits of cheese or sausage are ideal. Make sure that your dog isn't distracted by anything before you start. Then click the clicker once. When your dog looks at you (as he will), hold out a treat. Now you've got his attention, click again. He'll look at you. Give him a treat. After five or six repetitions, he'll be beginning to get the idea, so ask him to do something he knows already – 'sit', or 'down'. As soon as he does it, click and give him a treat.

It may sound almost too simple, but it works. Try not to talk while you're practising clicker work (other than to say 'good dog' as you hand your dog his treat if you really find not speaking too hard) and, as with all types of training, keep each session short and end it before your dog gets bored. Once your dog has the idea, you'll find that as soon as he hears the click, he starts looking to you for his treat. When this happens you can leave it a moment longer before you reward him. When he has a behaviour fully learned, you can

gradually stop treating and use just the instruction and the clicker, then praise him – and move onto the next thing you'd like him to learn.

If you're impressed with the results that even one or two sessions of clicker work have achieved with your dog, look for a local class that you can attend together to take it further.

# Learning to play

There are good and bad habits, even in play. We've already covered how to stop puppies nipping and jumping (see pages 122–3). Here we look at how you can control chase games, and at games that you should think carefully about playing at all.

Left: **Many dogs adore a game of 'tug'. Always ensure that you end up with the toy at the end of the game.**

## WRESTLING AND TUG

Many dogs love play-wrestling, whether with their owners or with other dogs. Dogs are well equipped to play-fight with each other as, provided the play is good-tempered, their skills are evenly matched: they all have four paws, and a mouth full of teeth, the latter normally used gently in dog–dog play. If one dog becomes over-excited and starts biting with too little inhibition, the resulting scuffle can usually be broken up without too much damage done. Dog–human wrestling can be a lot of fun too – but it's much riskier.

If the dog becomes over excited – as can happen in a second, far too fast for a human to bring things to a halt – an uninhibited bite will do much more damage to a human face than to a dog's, and even dogs who are usually very even-tempered are never one hundred per cent predictable.

However much fun it may be, behaviourists' advice on human–dog play-fights is usually simply 'don't', because the risks outweigh the pleasure. The fact is that dog bites can do serious damage, and a dog that has been over-stimulated to the point of biting may have to be destroyed.

Equally, most dogs love a game of tug. Tug is more controllable than wrestling, as the contact isn't direct and there is a 'third party' (the toy), which can be removed if things get out of hand. If your dog loves tug, stay in charge of the game and, when it finishes, take charge of the toy and put it away until the next session, rather than allowing your dog to carry it off as his prize.

## CHASING

Take care that you're always the one chased when you play. Most dogs can easily outrun their owners and you don't ever want to be chasing after your dog in a non-play situation. You'll have seen in dog–dog play that both chaser and chased have a great time, so if your dog runs away from you, simply turn and run as fast as you can in the opposite direction. Shout and whoop as you run to make it clear that you expect to be chased. No dog can resist the challenge, and he'll soon come chasing after you.

Below: **Hard-wired to love chasing games: it won't matter to your pet whether he's chaser or chased.**

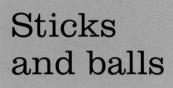

# Sticks and balls

Most dogs are naturally attracted to sticks and balls, whether they love to carry them or wait breathlessly for you to throw them so they can run and fetch. It's easy to throw something for a dog, but here are some ideas for extending the game.

### DOUBLE-FETCH

This game suits a dog that is reluctant to give up his stick or ball after he's fetched it. Simply arm yourself with a second toy and, when your dog returns to you after fetching the first, wave the new one in front of him. He'll drop the one he's holding to make a play for the second, and you can throw them in turn. If your pet tends to guard things that he treasures, pick up the toy he dropped and hand it right back to him. This will reinforce the idea that he'll only benefit from giving it up a next time.

**CHECKLIST**
**Throwing fun**

- If your dog is athletic, buy a ball-thrower. It will help you to throw the ball further.
- Tennis balls are best for throw and catch because they're durable and have good bounce. Light foam balls are a good alternative for young puppies or very elderly dogs.
- If your dog likes pushing rather than catching, buy some cones and try him on a mini-slalom course. Many dogs are quick to learn how to weave a ball if their owner demonstrates first.
- When you're playing Frisbee with your pet, don't throw too aggressively – remember, he has to catch the disc with his teeth, not his paws!

Left: **Few dogs can resist a ball game, whether it involves throwing, chasing or nose-to-nose tactics.**

## HUMAN-STYLE PLAY

Dogs can learn to enjoy all sorts of ball games, so don't limit yourself to fetch. Football, rounders and volleyball are all within the reach of a ball-mad dog. See what arises naturally in the course of a kickabout with your dog. Some dogs love to bounce a slightly larger ball off their nose, while

Right: **If your dog's a high-jump-and-catch enthusiast, the soft-edged type of Frisbee will be easier on his jaws.**

others seem to have natural, inbuilt dribbling skills.

To try rounders, first recruit a few players – a mix of people and dogs will be the most fun – and use a child's set with a light plastic bat and ball. Your dog probably won't understand the niceties of the rules, but if you get him to run along with a human player, the game is bound to be lively and enjoyable for everyone.

Volleyball is a more specialized skill, but if your dog goes nose- rather than mouth-first for a ball, he may pick it up. You'll need to set a low net up in the garden and, as you did for rounders, choose a light ball. Start a game with a (human) friend and see if your dog joins in. If he shows any interest, encourage him with high-pitched whoops.

These games are meant to be played for fun, at home, but if your dog shows a particular aptitude, you may have a candidate for flyball. Flyball is an organized game in which the canine competitors are required to jump a series of hurdles, set off a tennis-ball thrower with a paw movement, catch the ball as it flies out, then return over the jumps. It's fast and wonderfully exciting for the participating dogs, not to mention being excellent exercise. Many dog clubs and classes offer flyball as a training option.

# Hiding games

Dogs love to hunt out both people and toys, and you can create a variety of games around the search. One of the most intriguing aspects of these games is watching a dog find its quarry seemingly by smell alone.

Humans are accustomed to using their eyes to find things, and dogs can sometimes seem slow to spot something that, from a human viewpoint, is in plain sight. Hide an object out of the sight of both a person and a dog, however, and 90 per cent of the time the dog will find it before the human does.

## HIDE AND SEEK

If you make the object of a game 'find the person' rather than find the toy, even young puppies will join in. This is a game that you can use to train your dog to keep an eye out for your whereabouts when he's off the leash. It's useful to inculcate the idea in a young dog that you're not always going to be there the instant he looks around for you, as it will make him more inclined to 'check back' with you when he's otherwise engaged, and will help in developing his recall.

So when you're outdoors and your puppy is off the leash and engaged in exploring his surroundings, quickly hide nearby behind a tree or bush. Keep a lookout from your vantage point and when your puppy looks up and notices you're not there and starts looking around for you, whistle or call to him. He'll easily find you and you can make a fuss of him as he

Left: 'Find the person' can be a great game for a dog. If children are playing, make sure they don't put their faces right into a dog's face, though, as he may read this as a challenge.

does. As he grows older, you can develop the game by hiding in slightly harder-to-find spots and by staying silent while he's looking. Always make a big fuss of him when he finds you, though, just as you would praise him when he responds to your 'come!' call – discovering you should be the most enjoyable part of the game.

If your dog enjoys playing hide and seek with you, you can create some variations of it with friends. When you're out walking in woodland, for instance, get one member of your party to distract your dog while the others run off and hide from him. He'll love seeking people out one by one. It's also a game that you can play indoors on a rainy day with a bored and underexercised dog: get members of the family to hide behind doors, curl up behind furniture and so on, all over the house, then let your dog loose to go and look for them.

If you want to raise the excitement level and your dog is a squeaky toy enthusiast, you can arm the players with different toys and they can squeak them from their hiding places – guaranteeing an almost hysterical level of excitement. You can use this game to teach 'go find!' as a command. If you say it just at the moment you let him loose, he'll quickly pick up what it means.

## HUNTING FOR OBJECTS

What's your dog's favourite activity? If he enjoys figuring things out, you could hide a loved toy under one of two or three upside-down boxes while

Above: **Rather than leaving your garden to the mercies of your dog's digging, give him somewhere special where he's allowed to dig instead.**

he's out of the room, then lead him in and ask him, 'Where's your toy?' If he doesn't get the idea straightaway, pretend to look for it yourself, under the furniture, behind cushions and in cupboards, before finally landing on the hiding place and discovering the toy with much fanfare. Repeat the exercise a few times and your dog will soon head into the room with enthusiasm and start hunting.

If your dog loves digging and you want to indulge him, you could make him his own sandpit, just like a child's play one. Not only can he dig there safely (better than in the flower beds or under the fence), but you can bury toys and treats in it and encourage him to dig them up.

# Basic agility

If you have a clever dog that needs a lot of exercise and plenty to keep his brain occupied – this can apply to any breed or type, from a Chihuahua to an Irish wolfhound – you may be the owner of a natural agility star.

Most dog enthusiasts will have seen astonishing displays of professional canine agility on television. In its simplest form, 'agility' covers a range of activities, such as jumping hurdles, balancing along a beam and pushing through a fabric tunnel. Canine professionals must cover a course against the clock, but you can easily introduce your dog to some of the different elements that make up the agility test in the comfort of his back garden. Some agility activities are more challenging than others, and not all are suitable for every dog. The joy of home agility is that you can customize your course and create something that plays especially to your dog's strengths and that he will really enjoy.

## TRAINING AGILITY

Any dog that enjoys lively play will probably have already mastered some agility skills. Because of the sport's athletic nature, however, you need to be sure that your dog is reasonably fit before you start training him officially, and be sure that any jumps you set up for him aren't too high. Some pieces of equipment aren't suitable for home courses – don't ever encourage your dog onto a seesaw, for example (the ones you see on televised agility are specially made and weighted). Most trainers recommend that a dog shouldn't use

Left: **'Doggy dancing'** routines to music make up one of the newer disciplines for dog-owner interaction. If you and your dog already enjoy agility and want to vary your classes, give it a try to see if it's for you.

Above: **Agility can satisfy many breeds' need for both physical and mental stimulation.**

agility equipment before he's a year old; the demands it makes may be too great for growing bones and muscles.

If you want to build your own course and have enough space for four or five separate features, set them up in a mini-circuit in your back garden. If you don't have enough space, see if you can use a friend's garden, or sign up a couple of your dog's playmates and take your equipment to a park where they can practise together.

A first agility course might include two or three jumps, some weave poles, a designated space or low 'pause' table at which you ask your dog to 'stay' for a short time, a tunnel and perhaps a low balance beam. Set them up with some space between each, then walk your dog around the 'course', asking him to try a couple of jumps, weave in and out of the poles, push his way through the tunnel, 'stay' at the pause table or point, walk along the balance beam, and finish off with a final jump. When you've gone around the course a few times – offering plenty of encouragement and some of his favourite treats at the trickier points – and your dog has begun to get the idea, run around it with him.

When he's got into the swing of it, you can introduce a time element or, if he enjoys the company of other dogs, set up a playdate in which he and his friends can each go round the course and see who's fastest.

If he takes to agility happily, you could look into the possibilities of teaching him on a more demanding course (see pages 146–7).

(see pages 146–7).

## CHECKLIST
## Improvised equipment for garden agility

- **JUMPS.** These should be very low at first – no higher than ten centimetres (4 in). As your dog gets used to them, raise them, but never higher than the dog's shoulder height. Use a piece of dowel or plastic tubing that can easily be knocked off if the dog hits it, balanced on cones or boxes at each end.
- **WEAVING POLES** are easily improvized using small plastic cones that you can buy at a toyshop.
- **COLLAPSIBLE TUNNEL.** A tunnel made of light polythene fabric with a rigid hoop entrance, which again can be bought at a toyshop.
- **PAUSE TABLE.** Any small, low outdoor table, or even a low piece of board.

# Professional agility

Agility is one of the most popular competitive sports for dogs. Full agility courses and competitions are organized and run by many local clubs and the most talented dogs may even compete at national level.

Agility is a test both of the dog's skill at completing a course without errors and to a set time limit, and of the bond between dog and owner as the owner guides the dog to success.

## A NATURAL TALENT?

If your dog has proved quick to train, grasps new games fast and enjoys performing for an audience, then look into your local dog training classes and clubs to see if there's a full agility course you can try him on.

Size isn't important: competing dogs are measured and entered into one of three size classes – small, medium or large – and the course obstacles are then amended in height and width according to which class is competing.

Most clubs won't allow a dog to compete until he is at least 18 months old, and many run special veteran classes, meaning that your dog can compete against older dogs as he ages.

## RUNNING THE COURSE

If you decide to take up agility seriously, precision in running the course becomes very important. Your dog will need to learn not only to get over, under and through all the obstacles as fast as possible but also to tackle each correctly. Paw contact needs to be made with marked areas on the A-frame, the seesaw and the dogwalk, for example. Because dogs

Left: Agility challenges a dog's fitness and his thinking powers – and at competition level, the canine stars tend to be dogs that love noise and attention too.

## CHECKLIST
## Obstacles in agility

Courses vary and so do the number and type of obstacles. A professional course, though, may include any or all of the following:

**JUMPS.** A whole series, including ordinary hurdles, a staggered double jump (rising spread jump), a brush-topped jump (brush fence), a jump with a trough of water on the far side of it (water jump), a roofed jump (sometimes called a lych gate), a hanging ring or tyre (suspended ring jump) and a series of low jumps that the dog has to jump over in a single leap (long jump).

**PAUSE TABLE AND PAUSE POINT.** The judge will require the competing dog to lie and stay for a set time period at each pause station, whether it's a table (raised platform) or just a point in the course.

**TUNNELS.** These may be collapsible with a rigid ring at the opening, or rigid all along their length.

**WEAVING POLES.** A series of poles set into the ground at regular intervals, which the dog has to slalom or weave through.

**A-RAMP.** A steep, A-shaped frame made from hinged panels, which the dog has to climb over. His paws must touch points at the base of either panel, so he can't simply jump down from the top point.

**SEESAW** (also called the teeter-totter). This is carefully weighted for the contest. The dog is required to pause at the top before walking down the other side.

**DOGWALK.** A balance beam with ramps at either end.

**CROSSOVER.** A table with ramps leading up to it on each of its four sides. The dog must go up and down two ramps as specified by the judge.

need to think their way round agility courses, most find agility training tiring. If you're the owner of a dog that you've never been able to tire, however long his walks, agility may be the answer.

Left: **Not all dogs – even smart ones – are naturals for club agility classes. Some find the noise and attention too much. Even if your dog's a natural athlete, don't push him to perform if he isn't enjoying it. He may just prefer a quiet ball game at the park.**

# Problems that arise with play

Apart from the fact that you may grow tired of playing before he does, there are a few concerns that may arise while playing with your pet. Deal with any issues calmly and firmly. Your dog wants you to keep playing with him, so it's up to you to set the agenda.

If your dog is highly reactive, he may become over-excited and aroused during play and start to behave too roughly. Or your dog may become too serious about his toys and start 'resource guarding', instead of exchanging them freely and letting you take them from him. Another kind of dog may be relaxed and pleasant in play with people, but take games with other dogs too seriously, turning something that started as a good-tempered rough and tumble into a scrap.

Below: **An over-possessive dog may find 'swapping' more palatable than simply giving up his toy.**

## CHECKLIST
### Rules of good play

🐾 Put toys away between play sessions, except for those he plays with on his own.

🐾 If your dog plays too roughly, ask him to sit and wait until he complies before re-starting play. If he's still too rough, walk away. Don't make a fuss, just leave the game.

🐾 Use your voice to control the pace of play. To rev things up, make high noises; to calm things down, use a lower voice.

🐾 Don't let your dog get too focused on a single toy. Provide a range of toys and mix them up when you play.

🐾 Don't make boundaries between training and play. Your dog will learn best if you incorporate brief training sessions amongst games.

Above: **Some dogs find concentrating easier than others. Games such as 'fetch' that make dogs think can be useful in helping them to focus.**

## ESTABLISHING HOUSE RULES

Plenty of dogs play all their lives both with other dogs and with people without any problems. Many, though, find play so enjoyable that they suffer some loss of control. Operate a 'play code' with your dog (see checklist box, left). Watch him play with other dogs, too, to get used to his personal body language. You need to be able to spot the signs that tell you things are going too far, whether it's a paw raised over his playmate's back or a slight stiffening in his posture.

If your dog isn't playing by the rules, redirect his attention. If he's playing with you, make him take some time out; if he's behaving inappropriately with another dog, call both dogs to you and remind them that you're in charge – then by redirecting their play along more appropriate lines.

# Tricks for an audience

Many dogs take great joy in 'showing-off' and performing for an audience. If you're the owner of a canine exhibitionist, rather than leave it up to him to decide how he's going to get attention, it's a good idea to channel his energies into one or two tricks.

### PLAY DEAD

This one may take time for your dog to learn, but it is physically easy – even if your pet has a hefty physique or is stiff and elderly. The desired result is that the dog be lying on his side, completely still. But before you can show a dog how to 'play dead', he first needs to learn how to 'rollover'. Once he's learned 'rollover' and gets it right every time, you can move on to the 'play dead' instruction.

To teach rollover, start by asking your dog to go into a 'down'. As soon as he's lying down, take a treat and bring it around the side of his head, so that he looks up, and then down the other side. As he turns his nose to follow the treat, his body should follow and roll over. This may take some practice to get right, although rolling over is something that's in a dog's natural repertoire, so as soon as he understands what you want he will do it quite happily. Only reward him when he manages to roll over.

Practise rollovers with your dog for a week or two before moving on to

'play dead'. To get him to play dead, ask him to rollover then, just as he's reached the midway point and is lying on his side, say 'Wait!'. As he pauses, say 'Play dead'. Practise this several times, treating at the exact moment your dog pauses. After a while, when he's playing dead successfully, you should be able to abandon the 'wait' and move straight to 'play dead' without pausing.

Below: **The challenge to the 'play dead' trick is to stop your dog rolling over completely onto his back – he should be on his side.**

## FETCH MY PHONE!

A dog that enjoys fetch games can usually be taught to fetch a specific object without much difficulty. 'Get my phone!' or 'Fetch the remote!' are good party pieces and will win him lots of applause.

This is a trick that's easiest to teach with a clicker (see pages 136–7) so that you can time the moment your dog gets it right very precisely. Put an object that your dog regularly plays fetch with on the floor along with your phone (your phone should be in a soft case, otherwise it's hard for your pet to pick up, and you don't want it covered in drool.)

Start by saying 'Fetch your ball!'. Your dog will probably pick up the toy he regularly plays with. Click as he does so. When he's identified his ball a few times, say 'Fetch my phone'. A quick dog may work out that it's the only other item there, but if after a couple of tries he isn't picking it up, kneel down and put it gently into his mouth while giving the instruction then, when he's holding it, click. Keep practising daily until he can identify both ball and phone every time. Then move away a

Above: 'Fetch my phone' is a great crowd pleaser, as well as being useful for a lazy owner.

little before you ask him to 'fetch', and he'll pick up the phone and bring it to you.

Once he's perfected these two tricks, he can perform them for your friends and you can lie back and bask in the applause.

## BASIC INSTINCT **Eyes and ears**

Dog are hardwired to act as much or more on what they see as on what they hear. Always remember that words have no intrinsic meaning for them, so if you're teaching tricks, keep your body language consistent with what your voice is saying. If you use hand signals to accompany your instructions, make sure that they are clear and distinct from one another. If your body is saying something different from the instruction that's coming out of your mouth, you can't expect your dog to know which instruction to act on.

# A healthy dog

The right diet, regular play and exercise are the
building blocks of your dog's good health, but they're
not the whole story. This chapter tells you what else
you need to know to care for your dog, from how to
deal with parasites and clip your dog's nails safely
to choosing insurance and conducting everyday
health checks. It covers home care and procedures
at the veterinarian, and sets out the complementary
health options that are now available to dogs as
well as people.

As part of an overview of canine wellbeing, from
puppyhood until old age, this last chapter also looks
at ways to cope with accidents and health problems.
It addresses the concerns around looking after a very
old or sick dog; how to decide when the point has
come to say goodbye; the grieving process, which
anyone who loses a well-loved pet must go through;
and moving on after a loss.

# Health basics

If you've owned a dog before, you'll probably be relaxed about keeping a new pet healthy. If your new dog is your first, however, and particularly if he's a rescue dog, you may worry more than you expected to about his day-to-day health.

## LEARN ABOUT YOUR OWN DOG

It may sound obvious, but dogs vary just as much as people, and what's right and normal for one dog may be a concern in another. If you're new to dog care, you may feel uncertain about the basics: how much water 'should' a dog drink each day, for example, or how tired 'should' he be after a long walk? The answer, of course, is that it depends on the dog. The only way you'll find out what's right for your dog in particular is to watch him over time and observe what seems to suit him the best.

Even experienced breeders, who have worked with a specific breed for many years, express surprise over how much individual dogs can vary, in terms of physical make-up and needs, as well as in behavioural issues. Learn to read your dog and to trust your judgement, and you'll be the first to know if something isn't right. Lethargy is the most universal sign that there's something wrong – and even if your dog is naturally quiet and shy, you won't need to be an expert to spot it. Sudden changes in behaviour can also be a pointer that there's something physically wrong. If Rex, who's always been so good about being handled, starts to growl when you try to brush his paws, it's unlikely that he's developed an aggression problem – there's probably something wrong with them.

Left: Wet nose? Check. Shiny coat? Check. Bright lively eyes? Yes. If your dog looks healthy, chances are that he is.

Right: **If a dog that's usually full of life suddenly wants to rest all the time, and seems to tire more easily than usual, there's something wrong.**

## WHEN TO CONSULT THE VETERINARIAN

The cost of veterinary visits makes some owners reluctant to take their dogs except in an emergency. While it's not sensible to rush to the veterinarian over every tiny concern, don't leave an obvious problem too long. If a dog vomits just once or twice, for example, skip a meal and then try again, but if he has persistent vomiting and diarrhoea, he could get tired and dehydrated within a couple of days unless he is given professional treatment. With a puppy or an older dog with compromised health or known problems, it's best to err on the side of caution.

Puppies in particular can become very ill very quickly (and can, with the right treatment, often recover just as fast), so play safe and consult a veterinarian within 24 hours if your puppy is evidently unwell.

## BASIC INSTINCT **Going to ground**

When a dog is hurt or isn't feeling well, he will do what a wild animal would and try to hide himself away. This may mean that he doesn't want to leave his basket or crate or, more extremely, will go behind or under a piece of furniture – somewhere where it is quiet and dark. This behaviour is purely instinctive: wild animals hide if they are sick to prevent predators from finding them and taking advantage of their weakness. If your dog is hiding away in corners, never try to drag him out forcibly because you'll probably get bitten. Instead, coax him out patiently and have a look at him to see if there's an evident problem. If there isn't, but he's unhappy, add some extra padding to his crate or basket so that he can make a nest (sick dogs often want to 'burrow' as it makes them feel more secure). If he's still hiding after 24 hours, take him to the veterinarian.

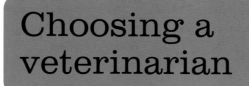

# Choosing a veterinarian

Chapter three (see pages 92–3) touched briefly on the importance of finding the right veterinarian for your dog. Having a sympathetic professional on hand will become increasingly crucial as your pet grows older.

For a young, healthy dog, a visit to the veterinarian's may be no more than an annual occurrence, but as your dog ages and health concerns inevitably begin to emerge, the visits are likely to increase in frequency.

Veterinary care is expensive, so take your time over choosing and don't forget that you're the customer and that you're entitled to ask questions before you sign up to the service. Ideally, start with a recommendation, but bear in mind that a veterinarian who suits a friend or colleague may not necessarily be

right for you, so make your own checks, too, and, if possible, ask if you can take a tour of the facilities to assess the conditions.

Good veterinarians have a rapport with animals as well the know-how to look after their health. Watch how the veterinarian handles your pet: a good one will be gentle and confident, and reassuring with a shy or nervous dog. If you're interested in complementary therapies or treatments, ask for the veterinarian's opinions on these.

While there are a few veterinary practices that use complementary treatments exclusively they are still quite rare. Most practices will refer you to complementary therapists if you ask (and many have relationships with external veterinary osteopaths, homeopaths and other types of holistic practitioners to whom they will refer you for specific problems).

Left: **Just like people, dogs will tend to visit the 'doctor' more frequently as they age. As your dog becomes a veteran, it's more important than ever that your veterinarian be someone you trust.**

🐾 The waiting room and all other areas should look clean, tidy and well-kept.

🐾 Both the desk staff and the veterinarians should be friendly, approachable and able to answer any questions.

🐾 How many veterinarians work at the practice? Who would take over if your own veterinarian was away?

🐾 Check that the veterinarian's qualifications are from a recognized veterinary college or institution and that he or she is certified with an appropriate association. Look up any qualifications that you don't recognize on the internet to confirm their legitimacy.

🐾 What are the surgery hours? Can you always get an appointment on the day that you call?

🐾 What are the arrangements for emergency care and attending surgery?

🐾 Who is at the surgery overnight? You'll want to ensure that the surgery is manned overnight as well as by day, ideally by a veterinary nurse or veterinarian, in case there are emergencies with pets left in overnight.

Above: **A good veterinarian should be able to establish a rapport with your dog and to deal gently with a dog who's frightened by a veterinarian visit.**

## PET INSURANCE

Pet insurance can be a bit of a lottery. If you adopt an elderly dog or one with established health problems, you may find either the premiums on a policy that will cover him are prohibitively expensive, or that the policies available exclude cover for his ongoing condition. On the other hand, if you have a young, fit dog, a policy that covers most contingencies should be affordable, and it's good to know that, should your dog need an emergency operation or be involved in an accident, you will be covered.

Discuss the pros and cons of different types of policies with your veterinarian, and ask about the cost of specific situations – for example, if your dog were to need surgery – to get a full picture before you decide whether or not to pay for full cover.

# Puppy health issues

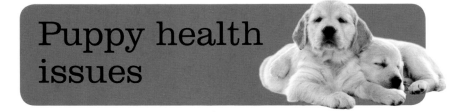

Two important issues will come up when you first take a puppy or a new dog to the veterinarian (see also pages 92–3). The first will be vaccination and the second will be whether to have the dog neutered, if it hasn't already been done.

## VACCINATION

The initial series of vaccinations for your puppy will only be completed when he is around four-and-a-half months' old. This is because your puppy is born with some immunity to various conditions, and this is subsequently strengthened by his intake of colostrum, the rich milk that is provided by his mother during the first few days of life. While maternal immunity is in force, the immunity provided by injections cannot fully 'take', so a series of shots is needed to ensure your puppy is fully protected as his natural immunity gradually decreases.

Many of the diseases that vaccination protects against are canine killers. Parvovirus, hepatitis and canine distemper are all very serious and can be fatal in a puppy, and sometimes even in an older dog. Leptospirosis, Lyme disease and parainfluenza (a contributor in the condition known as 'kennel cough') are other illnesses that may be vaccinated against, and rabies is another that may be judged

necessary depending on your dog's circumstances and where you live (rabies shots are mandatory in some countries). Most veterinarians give combination shots – that is, single injections that administer the required vaccines in combination.

While professionals agree that vaccination is necessary to build your puppy's immunity at first, there's a growing debate as to whether dogs need annual boosters, or as many combination shots as have been commonly been given over the last couple of decades. Some people believe that boosters every two or three years are sufficient to keep their dogs' immunity at a safe level; others feel that fewer combination shots should be given, arguing that these in themselves compromise a dog's health and have side-effects, and that individual injections are better for the dog. These arguments have not been proven 'right' or

Right: **Puppies are particularly susceptible to some illnesses, so it's important to take care with their vaccination schedules,**

'wrong', so ask your veterinarian for current advice about inoculations and about the pattern of shots that the practice usually gives.

## SPAYING OR NEUTERING

Neutering (also called spaying for a female dog) is the process that will render your pet sterile. Neutering a dog involves removing his testes; neutering a bitch is a larger operation that entails the removal of her ovaries and uterus. Both are surrounded by a lot of stories and myths, not all of them true.

Mainstream current advice is that if you don't want to breed from your dog, you should have him or her neutered at a relatively early age. In the past it was thought that a bitch should be allowed to have her first season or even one litter of puppies before being spayed; today, veterinarians will often suggest neutering for both sexes at around six months.

The operation usually entails an overnight stay at the veterinarian's. Recovery is faster in dogs; bitches may need to be kept quiet for a week or so.

## CHECKLIST
## Pros and cons of neutering

- Owners of bitches won't have the inconvenience of dealing with a season twice a year.
- In the case of dogs, some argue that neutering reduces aggression or a propensity to fighting.
- Neutered dogs can be more prone to obesity, although this can be controlled by limiting a dog's diet and keeping up a good level of exercise.
- In both dogs and bitches, neutering reduces the probability of certain cancers occurring in later life (prostate, uterine and breast cancer among them), although some current research suggests that it may slightly increase the chances of other health problems.

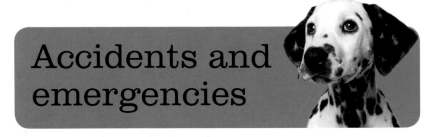

# Accidents and emergencies

Of course it's preferable to anticipate and avoid accidents and emergency situations, but it is not always possible. Here's how to plan ahead, together with some first-aid tips, so that you're as prepared as you can be when the worst happens.

There are many things you can do that will help to keep your dog safe, and so avoid potential heartache. Some of the advice will seem obvious, but you'd be surprised how often mistakes are made, leading to dogs getting lost, hurt or both. Even if you are a careful owner, read the checklist of safety habits, opposite.

## MICROCHIPPING

If your dog is microchipped, you greatly increase your chances of getting him back if he gets lost or goes missing. Most veterinarians and many rescue organizations offer an inexpensive microchipping service.

The procedure is simple: a minute electronic chip, smaller than a grain of rice, is injected under the skin of your dog's back, between his shoulder blades. It holds a number that is referenced on a national database. Should he ever be lost, his chip can be read through a scanner and he can be traced back to you.

## CAUSES OF ACCIDENTS

The commonest emergency situations for dogs are being hit by a car, poisoning, burns, bloat and heatstroke. Shock may occur on its own or be a complication in any of these. Whatever the problem, the first thing to do is check that your

Left: **It's fast, easy and painless to get your dog fitted with a microchip, so it's worth considering, particularly if he spends a lot of time running free.**

dog's airways are clear and that he is still breathing. Cardiopulmonary resuscitation (CPR) can be practised on dogs, but unless you're trained in human resuscitation and are used to the drill it's probably best to concentrate your efforts on getting the dog to professional help as fast as possible.

If you are trained in CPR, put something around the dog's muzzle to keep his mouth closed and breath only through his nose, rather than practising mouth-to-mouth as you would for a person.

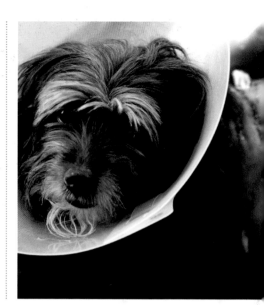

Right: **Recovery can take time. When a dog has bad wounds, he may have to wear a plastic 'Elizabethan' to make sure that he doesn't worry at them.**

## CHECKLIST
## Good safety habits

- Check your dog's collar and leash every few weeks to ensure that they are still sturdy and don't have the sort of wear that could cause them to give or break.
- Don't leave your dog tied up in public places while you run errands. Dogs can be stolen even when you think they're in your sight.
- Train your dog carefully to stay in the car after you open the door until he gets a word from you – a dog leaping out into the path of traffic is a common cause of accidents.
- If you have a front door or a gate that opens straight on to the street, train your dog in the same way, so that he stands aside to let you go first rather than rushing out.
- Store your veterinarian's emergency number on your mobile phone. If you leave your pet with a friend or carer, make sure they not only have the veterinarian's name and number but also know the route to the surgery in the case of a health emergency.
- If you don't do so already, keep a first-aid kit both at home and in your car. You can put together a special one for dogs, but most of the contents of a standard first-aid kit can be pressed into service to treat dogs as well as people.

- Act quickly: every second counts.
- If the dog is conscious, improvise a muzzle before touching him; if he's in pain and confused, he may bite. You can loop any soft piece of cloth loosely around his muzzle, under his chin and behind his ears. If he's choking, ask someone to hold his jaw while you conduct a quick sweep of his mouth and throat to remove any blockage, and pull his tongue forward so that he doesn't choke on it before attaching the improvised muzzle.
- If your dog is bleeding heavily, make a pad from any fabric you have – a t-shirt or shirt, for example – and apply it to the wound with a firm, even pressure.
- Call the veterinarian's emergency number on your phone to warn the surgery that you are coming. If the veterinarian can come to the phone, describe what happened so that the surgery can be prepared to act as fast as possible as soon as you arrive.
- Lift the dog onto the backseat of a car, while moving him as little as possible. If you can, place him on a flat surface, such as a large piece of board, first. If he has any obvious breaks or injuries, try to keep that part of his body as still as you can.
- Ideally, someone who isn't driving should sit next to the dog and tend to him during the journey to the veterinarian's.

## POISONING

Symptoms of poisoning vary, from extreme vomiting and diarrhoea to very fast or slow breathing, dilated pupils and even fitting. Unless you are certain what the poison was, it's best not to attempt treatment yourself. A caustic poison, for example, shouldn't be vomited up, as it can do even more damage, while other poisons need to be got out of the system – usually by means of vomiting – as soon as possible.

If you know what the poison was, speak to your veterinarian and ask if there's anything you should do, but be prepared to get him to the surgery as soon as possible.

## SHOCK

Shock can result from a whole range of causes, from trauma or poisoning to heavy blood loss. It results from a disruption to the dog's circulation; as blood fails to reach the body's organs, its functions start to shut down.

Symptoms may include dry mouth and lips, and pale gums, cool feet and muzzle, evident weakness and a rapid heartbeat. Your dog may seem confused and anxious, and in extreme cases can fall unconscious.

It is essential that shock is treated professionally: try to keep your dog calm, talk to him in a reassuring tone and get him to the veterinarian as fast as you can.

## BURNS AND HEATSTROKE

If the burn is confined to a small area and is not too serious, cool the area with water (cool, not icy cold), then apply a soothing cream. If the burn is more serious, get your dog to the veterinarian. You shouldn't put anything directly on the area, although you can trickle cool, not cold, water over it. Tent a clean towel over it during the trip to the surgery, but don't let it touch the skin.

Dogs are particularly vulnerable to heatstroke because they cannot sweat through their skin. Symptoms include rapid panting, thick saliva from the mouth and, inside the mouth, deep red gums. Get your dog to a cool place as fast as possible. Offer cool (not cold) water, and soak towels in cool water and drape them around his head and feet. Use cool water, not cold; over-rapid cooling can cause constriction of the blood vessels and make the problem worse. Take him to the veterinarian to be checked over, even if he seems better.

## BLOAT

Bloat needs to be recognized and treated professionally, as it can happen fast and may be fatal. It is caused when the stomach becomes filled with air (usually after a large meal) and twists in on itself. This rapidly causes complications as the blood flow to the heart is constricted and the dog may go into shock. A dog with bloat can't be treated at home and needs to be taken to the veterinarian as soon as possible.

If you own a breed that's susceptible (typically large dogs with deep chests, such as Dobermans or German shepherds are the most prone to the condition), you will probably have discussed it with your veterinarian already. Susceptible dogs should not be exercised for some time after a meal to avoid the condition occurring.

Below: **Provided that a dog is got to the veterinarian and treated fast, he may recover surprisingly fast even from serious emergencies.**

# Additions and supplements

Whether or not it is necessary to add vitamins, minerals or other supplements to a dog's diet has become one of the most hotly debated subjects within canine care, even between professionals.

Some hold that a dog that is given adequate amounts of healthy food shouldn't need any supplementary help. This in itself opens an argument, because there's little doubt that many commercial dog foods are stripped of their original vitamins and minerals during the many processes they must undergo – making it more likely that some supplemental nutrition will be necessary if a dog is exclusively fed this food. Others believe that an all-round supplement can be beneficial for every dog, and that specific additions can help with some long-term chronic conditions. The difficulty with this argument is that the needs of dogs in terms of vitamins and minerals are quite different from those of humans' (so dogs shouldn't be given supplements produced for people – too much vitamin D, for example, can be dangerous for dogs, while the 'necessary' dosage for a dog is much lower than that for a human).

Supplements for dogs, which are heavily advertised, are also sold without any controls, which means dog owners must simply trust in the scruples of the manufacturers. If something you've read or heard from a fellow dog-owner makes you think that a supplement would benefit your dog, always consult your veterinarian before giving it to him, and stick to the most reputable brands.

Left: **If your dog is young, strong and fed the optimum diet, there may be no need to consider giving him supplements as well.**

## TREATING ARTHRITIS

Arthritis is very common in older dogs, and in particular those of the larger breeds. One of the few supplements that is almost universally agreed to be effective is a glucosamine/chondroitin mix, which has been widely accepted over the last 20 years as an alleviator of painful joints.

Arthritis is caused by the breakdown of cartilage in the joints and can result in a disabling level of pain. Glucosamine and chondroitin are both substances that occur naturally in dogs' bodies, but older dogs can have trouble creating the amount of glucosamine that they need. Glucosamine, taken as a supplement, is helpful in encouraging the body to replace cartilage (which can be done naturally), while chondroitin provides a rearguard action against some enzymes – which, again, occur naturally in the dog's body, and which work towards the breakdown of cartilage material.

In combination, in the right dosage, the supplement can offer a dog considerably more mobility in his later years. So if you have an older dog that seems stiff, gets up awkwardly and moves as though his joints are painful, ask your veterinarian if he might benefit from glucosamine supplements.

## PILLS

If your veterinarian has confirmed that a supplement or two will be beneficial to your dog, you need to be sure he takes them. The same goes for pills in general.

### CHECKLIST
### How to give a pill

- Place the pill within easy reach.
- Call your dog and ask him to sit alongside you.
- Put your left hand over the top of the dog's muzzle and align your fingers and thumb on either side of his top teeth. Squeeze slightly while gently pulling your dog's head up. His mouth will open a little.
- Acting fast, take the pill between the forefinger and thumb of your right hand, pull your dog's lower jaw down slightly with a free finger and pop the pill into your dog's mouth, as far back as possible.
- Press down – lightly – with your left hand and up with your right so that your dog's mouth closes. Hold his nose down slightly until he swallows.

While some dogs swallow down pills whenever they are asked, and others are happily prepared to take a pill provided it is presented in a small piece of meat or other treat, still others may be less relaxed, especially if it's been specified that the pill must be taken without food. If you're calm and firm, however, you can help your dog take his pill without a lot of fuss (see above).

# Dealing with parasites

Most dogs will be host to a parasite at some point in their lives, and a responsible dog owner is always on the lookout. It's best to identify the problem quickly, before it gets out of hand. Better still, you can take preventive measures to avoid it altogether.

## EXTERNAL PARASITES

If you brush and comb your dog regularly you will spot the early signs of any parasites. By far the commonest of all the parasites are fleas and ticks. When it comes to fleas, prevention is much easier than cure: a monthly treatment (either taken internally, in pill form, or as a liquid dropped directly onto the skin of your dog's neck) is available from your veterinarian and, used regularly, can ensure that he never gets fleas. Veterinarian's recommendations are best for flea treatments; some over-the-counter options from pet shops are of doubtful effectiveness.

If you suspect your dog does have fleas (the most obvious sign is that he'll scratch a lot), carefully deep-comb a thick part of his coat – at the back of his neck or just above his tail – onto a piece of dampened kitchen towel. Flea dirt shows up as black specks that redden when wet, so it's easily spotted. If you have to treat for present fleas, remember that you'll need to treat your pet's surroundings as well. Fleas live around your dog, rather than on him full time, so wash all bedding and spray carpets and soft furnishings.

Ticks are members of the spider family and, as well as drinking your dog's blood, can also be carriers of specific problems, such as Lyme disease, a serious bacteria-borne illness which can cause long-term arthritis, among other things, in both dogs and people. Ticks are very tiny when they attach themselves to your dog's skin – often less than a millimetre long – but they swell as they drink his blood and drop off when sated. You'll spot them before this, as a fully engorged tick can be

Left: **Fleas are very common; treatment against them must be thorough to succeed.**

left: External parasites can be eliminated with regular bathing and topical treatments applied to the skin.

the size of a pea and becomes obvious as you feel through your pet's coat. If your dog often runs through thick undergrowth or long grass, check for ticks every few days, including out-of-the-way spots such as between his toes and under his tail.

Some flea treatments are effective against ticks as well – ask your veterinarian about these if you find ticks regularly. Ticks should be removed carefully, with narrow tweezers that you can use to grasp them at the head. Pull hard but slowly until the tick comes away, then dab the spot with antiseptic cream. If you remove only part of a tick and the mouthparts remain in your dog, they may cause an infection.

Less commonly, dogs can suffer from mites. There are several types of these tiny insects – like ticks, also members of the spider family – some of which may give a dog mange or scabies. They are far less common than fleas or ticks; most types, among other problems, cause intense itching and can readily be diagnosed and

treated by your veterinarian. One specific, more common, type infects a dog's ears (see pages 168–9).

## INTERNAL PARASITES

Dogs can suffer from internal infestations of worms, usually passed on through eating or, on occasion, just sniffing and snuffling around something that contains active larvae. Some types of worm pose a more serious threat to a dog's health than others and, while they are hard to prevent, they are easy to treat. Heavy infestations of worms can be the cause of constant upset stomachs and a general loss of condition. Worming treatments must be regular (usually monthly for dogs) as there is no long-lasting solution.

By far the commonest internal pests are roundworms. Puppies are usually born with them (they can migrate between puppy and dam). If the puppy is given proper care and fed well they may reduce to negligible numbers as he matures, but some veterinarians believe that puppies should be wormed from two or three weeks of age anyway. More serious (though also much rarer) are whipworms and hookworms, both of which live in a dog's intestine.

Tapeworms are another possibility, particularly if a dog has had problems with fleas – some types of tapeworm eggs are transported by fleas, and dogs may ingest them. All these, however, can be dealt with straightforwardly once diagnosed.

# Everyday health care

Most of your pet's health care will be undertaken by, or on the recommendation of a veterinarian. However, there are some basic checks that can be carried out at home to make sure any problems are identified as early as possible.

Get used to having a good look at your dog on a regular basis and you'll be more likely to notice any changes in him – lumps and bumps that weren't there before; bad breath; cuts or abrasions on his feet and pads, to name just a few – that might give rise to health concerns. Just as with puppy handling, the more your dog is used to being handled and looked at, the less fuss he'll make when it's necessary.

## TOOTH CARE

Ideally, you should brush your dog's teeth every day, as you do your own. While it may not always be possible to accustom an older dog to this (and it's not a good idea to try on a nervous new arrival from the dog shelter), if you have a puppy or an amenable adult, it's a great habit to establish. Not only can it help to avoid gum disease and expensive tartar-scraping sessions at the veterinarian, but it also familiarizes you with your dog's mouth so that you'll later be able to see quickly if he has any problems.

You can buy several kinds of toothbrushes designed for dogs, including electric models, but the most commonly available type fits onto your fingertip so that you can easily work it all around your dog's mouth, including the back teeth. Use a dog toothpaste; the human kind is unsuitable for dogs, and you can choose a flavour such as beef or

Left: **A discharge in your dog's ears should be diagnosed and treated properly by the veterinarian.**

chicken, which may make him keener on the process. Start by rubbing a tiny amount of the toothpaste on your dog's gums. As he licks it off and appreciates the taste, you'll find that brushing gradually around his mouth, not neglecting the back teeth, will be straightforward.

If you can't brush your dog's teeth, at least try to ensure that he does some heavy-duty chewing, either on toys, such as rubber kongs, or on large beef bones. This will help to keep tartar at bay.

## EAR CARE

Checking a dog's ears is simple. Just look into your dog's ear holes under a good light, lifting the flaps if your dog has drop ears. The ear should be pink and clean, without discharge. If it's clogged with darker wax or has a discharge, there may be a number of causes – ear mites, trapped grass seeds, or an unrelated infection – and you should take your dog to the veterinarian, who can look deeper into the ear, diagnose the problem and prescribe treatment. Check the ears every time you groom your dog,

Above: **Clipping is necessary when the nails extend in front of the dog's toes.**

so that you catch any problems early on. Never poke around in his ears, but only check them visually.

## NAIL CLIPPING

Like toothbrushing, nail clipping can be done at home if your dog is used to being handled. If your dog walks a lot on hard surfaces, his nails may never need trimming. For dogs who run a lot on softer ground, however, the occasional trim is required: if the nails are extending well in front of the toes and touch the ground before his pads do, they need to be clipped.

To clip, hold your dog's paw gently but firmly with one hand and clip across each of the nails with the other, using purpose-bought clippers. If your dog has light-coloured nails, cut short of the quick, the blood vessel running down the centre of the nail, which is perceptible as a dark band inside the nail. On black nails, the quick can't be seen as a guide, so take care not to clip too close.

### WARNING

It's easy to nick the quick of a nail accidentally, and if you do it will bleed surprisingly badly. Keep some styptic powder on hand – available from pet shops or your veterinarian – and, if this happens, dab a little on the nail. Not only is it anti-bacterial, but it will also help to stop the bleeding.

# Complementary solutions

Just as interest has grown in holistic treatments such as acupuncture and herbalism as an approach to human health problems and conditions, so they have become an increasingly widely available and well regarded option for our pets too.

## WHAT IS HOLISTIC MEDICINE?

Allopathic medicine, also called conventional medicine, is the approach we are most familiar with in the West when it comes to treating both our pets and ourselves for physical complaints. Its defining principle is to treat the symptoms of disease as they arise. Its opposite number, holistic medicine – also called complementary or alternative medicine – comprises a wide range of disciplines which, put very simply, hold in common the idea that the underlying cause of the symptoms should be treated rather than the symptoms themselves, which conventional medicine might seek to suppress with drugs .

Today, most of the disciplines that humans call on to treat various conditions are available for dogs. There are canine specialists in homeopathy, herbalism, acupuncture, chiropractic medicine and osteopathy, to name just a few, and there are also some general holistic veterinarians who work to broad holistic principles themselves and who can make referrals to specialists working in the area that they feel may help your pet.

If you've always attended a conventional veterinary practice, the idea of acupuncture or herbal medicine for dogs may seem strange, but you can be assured that the

Left: **Specialists in herbal medicine may use many of the same herbs – such as gingko biloba – to treat both dogs and people.**

principles behind the treatments are well worked out and that practitioners are usually highly trained and qualified in the treatments they offer. There are many books exclusively dedicated to the subject of holistic care for pets (see the further reading section at the end of the book for some suggestions). If you are interested, read around the subject widely so that you can take an informed view about what treatments may be of benefit to your dog.

One aspect that many holistic practitioners are keen to stress is that their therapies may take a little time and that some experimentation may be necessary before they start to work effectively

Converts to complementary medicine feel that in general it lacks the downsides, and in particular the side-effects that are a disadvantage in many conventional drug treatments. If you want to try some holistic alternatives for a health problem in your dog, most conventional veterinarians will be able to offer a referral. Be aware, though, that not all holistic disciplines can be used in tandem with one another, and many holistic practitioners ask that you cease to use allopathic methods (such as prescribed drugs) for the duration of their treatment.

What follows is a brief overview of the mostly widely used disciplines of holistic treatment for dogs. It's far from exhaustive, but it will give you some idea of the range available and of the general thinking behind some of the treatments.

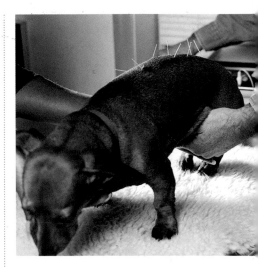

Above: **A specialist in chiropractic medicine or osteopathy will want to check your pet carefully, all over, before starting any treatment.**

## CHIROPRACTIC MEDICINE AND OSTEOPATHY

Chiropractic medicine operates on the principle that misalignments in the body's musculoskeletal system, particularly in the spine, affect the nervous system and in turn manifest themselves as health problems. It involves spinal manipulation of the vertebrae to encourage them back into their full range of movement. It has been used for many problems in dogs, from hip dysplasia to epilepsy.

Osteopathy is also a manipulation therapy, but the movements it employs are more varied, ranging from massage-like strokes of the soft tissue to 'clicking' the dog's joints. Osteopathy is commonly used in recovery from surgery, on working dogs with strains, and for general problems such as arthritis.

## HERBAL MEDICINE

As its name suggests, herbal medicine involves the use of plants in the treatment of health problems. Although many contemporary allopathic drugs have their origins in herbal treatment, herbalists believe that the plants are best used and are more effective in a more natural state. Some herbalists espouse traditional Western herb lore while others work within Chinese medicine. Both systems have their fans, but they are quite different from one another.

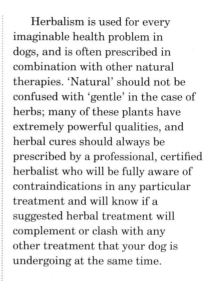

Herbalism is used for every imaginable health problem in dogs, and is often prescribed in combination with other natural therapies. 'Natural' should not be confused with 'gentle' in the case of herbs; many of these plants have extremely powerful qualities, and herbal cures should always be prescribed by a professional, certified herbalist who will be fully aware of contraindications in any particular treatment and will know if a suggested herbal treatment will complement or clash with any other treatment that your dog is undergoing at the same time.

## HOMEOPATHY

Homeopathy originated in Germany in the early 19th century. It is founded on the principle that giving the body a tiny amount of a substance that will produce the same effect as that which is making it ill will stimulate the body's healing mechanism to work to cure it. Homeopathic pills and powders contain infinitesimal quantities of these provoking substances, and are believed to act as triggers to the body to enable it to heal itself.

Left: **Many dogs enjoy a gentle massage, particularly if they are arthritic. Some specialists teach courses so that you can learn to massage your dog at home.**

Its effectiveness in animals is the very aspect of homeopathy that gives pause to sceptics voicing their doubts about it as a system.

Even if you don't believe in it, and feel that its efficacy in humans is brought about more because the patient wants to believe in it than in any innate value in the system, the fact that homeopathy has often been successful in treating horses or dogs certainly gives doubters something to think about.

## ACUPUNCTURE AND ACUPRESSURE

Acupuncture is an ancient discipline and an important part of Chinese medicine. It is believed to stimulate and adjust the energy flow through the body's pathways or 'meridians' by the use of, in acupuncture, very narrow needles and, in acupressure, simply the pressure of the fingertips.

It has a long and respected history in canine treatment and specialists use it for a huge range of conditions from skin problems to digestive complaints. There are many additional refinements possible to the treatment, including moxibustion, in which herbs are burned near the critical point on the energy meridian being treated, or even the use of ultrasound to help to clear the flow of energy.

To the surprise of their owners, many dogs accept the needles involved in acupuncture calmly and are relaxed under treatment. Most acupuncturists work over a course of two or more treatments to resolve a problem.

## CASE HISTORY
## Skin problems

At seven years old, Ted the terrier had a bad case of seasonal skin allergy. Every year, between May and September, he developed terrible itching. Left untreated he would scratch himself raw. His veterinarian had suggested cortico-steroids when he was two and ever since he'd been taking pills each summer.

Clare, his owner, was relaxed about this – the pills worked – until a friend alerted her to the steroids' potential side-effects. She was horrified to learn that they were implicated in all kinds of health problems later in a dog's life, from kidney failure to rheumatism. Asking for a recommendation from her veterinarian, and explaining her concerns, she visited a holistic practice. The methods didn't work straight away: a course of homeopathic remedies seemed to have no effect. But by trial and error, across several months, a change of diet and several acupuncture treatments gradually improved Ted's condition. Now, before the start of the allergy season, Clare takes him for two canine acupuncture sessions – and Ted no longer has to take steroids.

# Behavioural problems

At various points in this book, you'll have come across the advice to call in a trainer or a behaviourist. The help of a canine professional can be invaluable when a problem arises in your dog's behaviour that you feel unable to deal with.

## DOG BEHAVIOURISTS

Although there are many dog trainers working within a range of approaches, from the old-fashioned authoritarian to the more current behaviour-based regimes, until 15 or 20 years ago the term 'behaviourist' wasn't used much except in quite specialist circles.

Today, some of the professionals who help people with problem dogs are behaviourists as well as dog trainers. This means that they have trained in ethology – animal behaviour. They look at the natural behaviour of dogs and see how it can be pressed into service in teaching the pet who lives in your home.

Behaviourists often form an effective bridge in understanding between a dog and his owner, because they can see the way in which the dog is thinking as well as the human. Because it's a relatively new discipline, though, there are still comparatively few practitioners and finding a qualified behaviourist to help you with your dog's problems may be easier said than done.

It's probably best to check with a recognized assocation or society that should hold lists of suitably qualified people (see page 189).

Even if you can't find a certified behaviourist, try to use a trainer who operates from a knowledge of animal behaviour and incorporates it into their training practices.

It's a good idea to ask plenty of questions when you're looking around. If you're already concerned about how your dog behaves, you need to be sure that you've found the right person to help you.

Below: **Behavioural problems aren't limited to the larger breeds: smaller dogs can be equally difficult to manage.**

## WHAT'S THE PROBLEM?

How do you decide whether your dog's behaviour is a problem? Some difficulties are unambiguous: if your dog is aggressive with other dogs; if he is guarded or threatening with people; if he is excessively timid or suffers from separation anxiety when you go out; if he is terrified of any loud noise... all of these scenarios will reduce the quality of day-to-day life for you both so seek some help.

Lesser problems, such as occasional on-leash lunging, a reluctance to engage with other dogs, shyness with strangers, may leave you undecided: are these simply character traits or problems that need resolving?

Generally speaking, if you think there's a problem, there is one. But the 'problem' may well rest in a misunderstanding. Your dog may not

Above: **If your dog gets over-aroused when he plays, it may dissuade other dogs from interracting with him.**

have figured out what you want of him, or simply doesn't see any benefit in behaving in the way that you want him to. Living as they do in the human world, most dogs are clever enough and interested enough to work out how people operate.

If you have a dog that can't interpret human behaviour, you may have the start of a problem. Normally these misunderstandings can be resolved relatively quickly because, by reading what your dog is 'saying', a professional will be able to explain how to make it clear to your dog what you want, and how to make it worth your dog's while (by giving him more of whatever he values, whether that's treats, games or simply attention) to comply.

## THINKING AROUND YOUR PROBLEM

You can begin to help yourself at the same time as you call in the experts. The first thing a professional will do is ask for a full case history of your dog (covering background, general health, behaviour as a puppy and so on – it may be very detailed) and an account of the problem (if the behaviour happens predictably she may also ask you to film it while it is going on). Ask yourself some questions in advance. By thinking in detail about when the problem first arose and the circumstances around it, you may find clues that will help you to solve it.

## MEETING WITH A PROFESSIONAL

When you meet with either a trainer or a trainer/behaviourist, they will want to take a full history of your dog. They will often call for a physical exam, too, particularly if the behaviour seemed out of character for your dog. Some physical

### CHECKLIST
### Analyzing behaviour problems

**Ask yourself:**

- Is the problem a one-off or part of a pattern? For example, if your dog normally approaches other dogs looking nervous, with his hackles raised, and has now bitten another dog, he's simply taking existing behaviour one step further – it's not a one-off.
- Is your dog generally laid back/nervous/forward and confident? What makes you think this about him?
- What's your dog's background? Did you get him as a puppy or as an adult? If the former, how much do you know about his parents? If you got him from a shelter, how much did the staff there know about his background?
- How do you behave when your dog seems nervous or defensive? For example, do you talk to him, lead him away on the leash, or ask him to sit?

Left: **Not much will surprise a behaviourist: most have dealt with everything from separation anxiety to aggression or timidity.**

Above: Check that a problem *is* a problem before consulting a professional. Although these dogs are indulging in quite rough play, everything about their body language tells you that they're having fun.

conditions can manifest themselves as behavioural problems. A thyroid imbalance, for example, may emerge as apparent aggression. It's therefore important to check your pet's health.

If a physical problem is ruled out, the trainer will want to spend some time observing your dog, and will probably try to recreate a situation in which they can watch the problem in action, whether it's dog–dog aggression or nervousness/snappiness towards people. Try not to let this make you nervous; it's necessary to establish what's going on with your dog, and if there's a problem it's up to the trainer to deal with it.

After observation, you will be given feedback on what the trainer thinks the problem is, some ideas about what's causing it and some guidelines and a plan to help work through the problem. There will usually be at least one follow-up visit and maybe more, to see how things are working out.

## CASE HISTORY
## Meeting with a professional

Sonia had got her dog Buddy from the local shelter. A five-year-old lab/collie cross, Buddy had been the pet of an elderly woman and was handed in when she died. Buddy was sweet and gentle at home, but when Sonia took him out, he was highly nervous. He seemed terrified of being outdoors and wanted only to get home.

Sonia tried gentle urging and she tried dragging Buddy out, but nothing worked. Eventually she took him to her veterinarian and asked for a referral to a good trainer. The veterinarian agreed, but wanted to perform a full physical examination first – and found that Buddy had an infection in his middle ear, which seemed to have an effect on his balance. The veterinarian suggested they treated the infection first before looking at the behaviour. To Sonia's surprise, over the next fortnight Buddy's timidity outside gradually reduced. She and the veterinarian concluded that the fact that Buddy's balance had been compromised had made him scared of places he didn't know: the 'behaviour' problem had been physical after all.

# Keeping your dog young

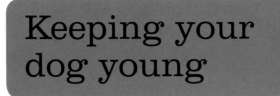

However long it's deferred, old age will arrive for your pet sooner or later. The rate at which your dog ages and the side-effects of ageing on his health and well-being will vary enormously according to the individual and his breed.

The first sign that your dog is ageing may be a slight slowing down in his capabilities and energy. Dogs who previously never tired, however long the walk or energetic the game, may seem less thrilled with long sessions of strenuous exercise.

This won't happen in the same way with every breed – just as large dogs can generally expect a shorter lifespan, so they will tend to age earlier. A breed that has a life expectation of nine or ten years, for example, may start to age at six or seven, while a breed with a longer expectation, of perhaps 15 years, may only begin to age perceptibly aged 10 or 11. Sometimes you'll notice small signs of ageing just as you would in a person. Your dog's muzzle may begin to turn grey, and he may begin to stand more solidly and have less 'bounce' in his step.

## KEEPING AN OLDER DOG ACTIVE

Just because your dog is visibly ageing, there's no reason he should stop learning. By all means let him set the pace when it comes to exercise, but explore other ways he can enjoy physical and mental stimulation. Dogs can play all their lives and you can tailor games to less athletic abilities. If your dog is no longer supple enough to jump after a ball or Frisbee, for example, find other games that he'll appreciate.

Contrary to the saying, you can teach an old dog new tricks and, provided that you've always had

Left: **Provided a dog is allowed plenty of downtime, most can remain active and playful well into old age.**

plenty of play and interaction with your dog, you can replace some of his more strenuous activities with others that will keep his mind active – even much older dogs can enjoy sessions of find the toy or hide-and-seek.

If your dog is one of the water-loving breeds, such as spaniels, Labradors or retrievers, swimming is still great exercise for him even if he's slightly arthritic, as the water will bear his weight. You should, however, be especially careful about what water he swims in: a dog that found strong currents easy when young may find them too challenging as he gets older.

## INTRODUCING ANOTHER DOG

Many owners opt to introduce a new puppy into the household as their existing pet ages. Thinking behind this varies, from 'it'll help to keep him young' to 'it will lessen the pain for us when we lose him'.

While it can sometimes be true that a new young companion can be a welcome playmate for a gregarious older dog, you should think things through before upsetting the status quo. It may be unfair to challenge a dog whose strength is just beginning to fail him by introducing a boisterous new puppy.

You'll also need the time and energy to provide clear leadership to both dogs, so that they know you are in charge and that what you say goes. If both you and your dog have been sinking into a rather comfortable middle age together, introducing another factor is going to shake things up, and you should expect and want this.

If after careful consideration, you do decide to take on a younger dog, it is important to guard your senior dog's privileges – whether they are a bed close to the radiator or having his meals served in a particular corner – so that he doesn't suffer any obvious loss of status from the introduction of a second dog into the household.

# Special diets

Reasons for feeding your dog a specially formulated diet vary. His needs may change as he gets older or he may have a particular health condition that calls for additions or subtractions to his food.

Whatever the reason, at some point in your pet's life, you'll probably find that you need to make some adjustments to his meals.

Of course, if you're feeding a home-cooked diet then any prescribed changes won't make too much difference, as you're already tailoring his meals. But even if you don't cook for him, there's a wide range of branded food sold to fit in with specific diets, from kibble for seniors to food for dogs with dental problems or kidney disease.

Probably the biggest favour you can do your pet as he grows older is to keep him at a healthy weight; obesity causes just as many problems in dogs as it does in humans. If your pet exercises less as he gets older, or for any other reason, he should be fed less too.

## DIETS FOR OLDER DOGS

Until comparatively recently it was thought that dogs should automatically be switched over to a 'senior' diet once they reached a certain age. Nowadays this thinking has changed, and the old 'senior diet' produced by pet food manufacturers – that is, one that is higher in fibre and lower in calories, with around a third less fat than the 'regular' type – is usually only recommended by veterinarians for dogs who need to lose weight or have problems with constipation or diabetes, and thus a need for more fibre. As your dog ages, however, it does become more

Left: There's nothing inevitable about an older dog becoming fat – after all, you're in charge of his diet!

important than ever to feed him high-quality food in which the nutrients are easily accessible to him. Cheaper branded foods may boast that they contain the ideal balance of protein, carbs and fats, but they often come in a form that isn't easily digestible for a dog (some of the sources of the 'protein' listed, for example, may be pulverized feathers and fur, not the tasty beef and chicken meat that are shown on the packaging). If you don't use a home-cooked diet, buy the best-quality branded dog food that you can afford, and ask your veterinarian or look up some discussion forums on the internet to get an idea of what's in the brands – they will give you more precise information than is ever found on a label.

Certain other conditions may demand changes in diet. Refined carbohydrates, for example, are implicated in the high incidence of diabetes in dogs, and part of the treatment for diabetic dogs is a high-fibre diet. Similarly, a dog's diet may have to be modified if he suffers

Above: **An older dog may need some tweaks and adjustments in his diet to stay healthy.**

from allergies. If your dog has a serious health condition, there will almost always be a case for amendments or augmentations – whether to his food or in the form of supplements – and you should manage his diet in collaboration with your veterinarian.

# Keeping an ageing dog

If your dog has moved from 'ageing' to definitely 'old' – which can be any age between eight and fourteen – you need to look out for him more carefully than when he was young and fit. Now is the time you can repay him for the enjoyment he's given you.

## HEALTH CHECKS

Now your dog is a pensioner, you may find that your visits to the veterinarian become more frequent. This can be for a whole range of reasons, even if your dog is generally in good health. Most veterinarians recommend six-monthly visits, as minor health concerns tend to crop up more often in an old dog.

You are the best placed to monitor your older dog's health.

Below: **Check that your older dog's sleeping place has plenty of padding to ease his ageing joints.**

Be punctilious about regular and thorough grooming sessions: not only will they help to keep your dog comfortable, but they're also the best way to spot changes in your dog's body that may be indicative of a larger health problem.

## KEEPING YOUR DOG COMFORTABLE

If your dog enjoys being handled, consider learning how to give him a massage. Learned properly and done gently and carefully, a massage session can relieve stiffness and

aches and pains, just as it can for a person, and many dogs love it. There are plenty of books available that will teach you, or you can find a local practitioner to show you how.

Allow for your dog's increased difficulty in moving around. You may need to lift him in and out of the car (or, with larger breeds, acquire a ramp that lets him get in and out himself without jumping). At home,

ensure that his bed and resting places are warm or cool enough – he'll become more sensitive to temperature with age. Even if he's been accustomed to resting on hard surfaces, he may enjoy something padded now. Look for a soft basket with thick quilting, or line a hard one with an old quilt; he will find it much more comfortable, particularly if he suffers from arthritis.

## CHECKLIST
## What to look out for

Check the following when you're grooming your older dog, and report any significant changes to your veterinarian:

- His teeth should look clean without too much plaque build-up, and his breath should smell fresh. Gum disease is common in older dogs, and can lead to the loss of teeth. It can also be an indicator of more serious underlying health problems. Look all around your dog's mouth when you brush, checking for sore spots and ulcers, as well as checking the teeth themselves.
- Check that his paws are clean, that the pads look elastic and the nails are the right length. Pads may thicken in older dogs, and this can be uncomfortable for them. They can be treated with special moisturisers, which you can get from the veterinarian. If your dog is walking less, his nails may need clipping even if his level of exercise previously made this job unnecessary.
- Check his elbows for areas of hard skin. These aren't necessarily painful but, again, moisturizer can help to keep his skin supple at such pressure points.
- As you groom, check the whole body for lumps and bumps. Older dogs may develop harmless cysts or fatty lumps on almost any part of their body. Although the vast majority are benign, you should always get new lumps checked by your veterinarian.
- Check the quality of his coat. Previously glossy coats may become a bit duller and thinner with age. An oil supplement may be useful in improving its condition – again, get a recommendation from your veterinarian rather than buying one direct from the pet shop; supplements vary considerably in quality.

# Very old or sick dogs

The last year or two of your dog's life may call for constant adjustments on your part. It's hard to watch a well-loved pet age, but there are many ways to make his old age enjoyable as well as reasonably comfortable.

## A WATCHING BRIEF

The only way to ascertain that a really old dog still has a good enough quality of life is to keep a close watch on him. While he was well and strong you didn't have to keep checking on where he was and what he was doing, but now you need to keep a much closer eye. In some ways it's like returning to his puppyhood: he'll probably need to be let out more often to avoid accidents in the house (and very old dogs may have some accidents anyway, not because they've 'forgotten' their house-training, but because, like small puppies, they simply can't keep it in); it's probable that he'll sleep more, and he may be less attentive to you too.

Look out for everyday ways you can help your dog. If he used to spend the evenings sitting beside you on the couch and he starts to go to his basket instead, offer to lift him up to his usual spot – the change may simply mean that he can't jump up any more. Similarly, a dog that loved to chew may no longer be able to cope with bones, but something a bit softer may still be palatable for him (pet shops sell various kinds of chewsticks suitable for older dogs).

It's easier on him if his surroundings and activities can remain familiar: keep his basket,

Left: With care and attention old dogs can still enjoy life – but it may call for more effort on your part.

crate, and anywhere else he uses as a resting place, as organized as they've always been, and try to keep as much of his routine in place as you can. Play for a very elderly dog might be as simple as rolling a tennis ball gently along the floor towards his nose and encouraging him to nudge it back to you, but that doesn't mean that he'll enjoy it any less.

Watch, too, for changes in behaviour. If you're grooming regularly (as suggested on pages 182–3) you should pick up evident physical changes, but the signs of changes in his mental state may be more subtle. Elderly dogs may become vague or appear confused.

A number of conditions can lead to this: deafness may mean that your dog 'startles' easily, as may failing eyesight (if you don't see something, it can sneak up on you), but some other signs such as excessive anxiety, gazing into the distance for prolonged periods and apparently ignoring you can be indications of a whole range of conditions. Old dogs sometimes suffer from CCD, or canine cognitive dysfunction, colloquially known as 'Doggy Alzheimers' because it causes similar symptoms to Alzheimers in people. It cannot be cured but, if correctly diagnosed, drugs can be used to reduce some symptoms.

Always consult your veterinarian about any noticeable change in your old pet's behaviour, and be ready to give detailed descriptions of exactly what you mean, as this will make it easier for your veterinarian to give an accurate diagnosis, and therefore prescribe the right treatment.

Above: **Dogs that need to be helped in and out of the car will often still love to look out as you drive.**

## TOWARDS THE END

Whether your dog is old and failing or is ill with an incurable condition, there may come a time when, in consultation with your veterinarian, you decide that he won't be getting better. This doesn't have to mean his life is over, but simply that you aren't trying to cure him. You can keep him content and comfortable by means of whatever treatment is available, from painkillers to visits from his friends, canine or human.

Whether this phase lasts for months or, as is more usual, a week or two, make time to be with him, and take some pictures as a memento of his later life. Ask your veterinarian for an honest opinion about your pet's quality of life, so that you can take action if it's no longer possible to keep your dog in tolerable comfort.

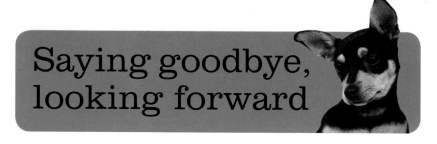

# Saying goodbye, looking forward

The majority of pets today do not die naturally but are peacefully euthanized. Most owners, therefore, find that the hardest part of watching their pet grow old and ill is deciding the point at which he should be put to sleep.

## CHOOSING THE TIME

If your dog is now very ill, your veterinarian may advise you that it's time to let him go. If on the other hand, he's functioning but old and rather unwell, the decision will usually be left to you.

If he isn't in great pain, but you feel that the time is coming, give yourself a few hours or sleep on your

decision. When you've made up your mind that his quality of life is compromised to the point that it's time to act, go through the checklist below to ensure you've thought through the details.

Most veterinarians will come to your home to euthanize your dog, if you prefer this. This means your pet will be in familiar surroundings and you won't need to move or disrupt him, and the experience may be less distressing for you too.

If you decide on a surgery appointment, the veterinarian will probably suggest a quiet time at the very beginning or end of the day to ensure that you don't have to wait.

The procedure is very simple: the veterinarian will give your dog an injection (sometimes preceded by a sedative) and shortly afterwards your pet's heart will stop. You will be asked if you want to stay with your dog. This is a matter of personal

Left: **Letting an old friend go is always a wrench. Keep plenty of photos and mementos to remind you of the good times you shared with your pet.**

choice, but most people opt to be there so that they can hold their dog through his last minutes.

After your pet's death, give yourself some time before you think about getting another dog. If you don't, you may find that you're looking for a dog that's identical to the one you've just lost, which is an impossible brief: far better to accept a new pet for his own personality and qualities than to look for a 'shadow' of your old, well-loved companion.

If you had your dog for a number of years, review your circumstances to see if what you can offer and what you need from a dog has changed before you decide on a new pet.

## CHECKLIST
### Before you say goodbye

**Having a well-loved dog put down is always upsetting. Think through these points before you make the final call to the veterinarian to make it as easy on both you and your dog as possible:**

- Decide where you would like to have your pet put down.
- Have a blanket or rug ready for your pet to lie on and to wrap his body in.
- Discuss payment in advance of the visit, and either pay then or ask if the veterinarian can bill you later – don't be unprepared for how upset you'll feel directly after your pet has died.
- If your pet is to be euthanized at home, decide where he will feel most comfortable. His bed, a favourite chair, or even a corner of the garden on a warm day may all be appropriate.
- Think ahead about whether you will be burying your pet (the choice of many people who have a garden that is big enough), or if you will ask the veterinarian to have him cremated (and, if the latter, if you want the ashes to be scattered or buried). If you decide on a burial, sort out how

you're going to prepare a grave beforehand. Don't underestimate how large and deep a grave is necessary for a big dog, and arrange for help to dig it if necessary.
- If you've chosen a home visit, consider whether you want to spend some time with your dog afterwards, and arrange in advance what will happen when this private time is over. You may find that a few hours with your pet's body helps you get used to the idea that he's gone. If you have another dog or dogs, some people believe they may accept the death of their companion more readily if they see the body – although a dog's reaction to death is unpredictable: some dogs seem serious and respectful, others treat another dog's body as an object, and don't seem to recognize it as their late housemate.

# Further reading

There's a huge range of titles available, offering everything from insights into behaviour to tips on effective training and information on alternative health for dogs. Here's a selection of some of the best.

The Body Language and Emotions of Dogs
**Milani, M M 1986**

Bones Would Rain from the Sky: Deepening Our Relationships with Dogs
**Clothier, S 2002**

Canine Body Language: A Photographic Guide to Interpreting the Native Language of the Domestic Dog
**Aloff, B 2005**

Dog Language: An Encyclopedia of Canine Behaviour
**Abrantes, R, Rasmussen, A and Whitehead, S 2001**

The Dog Listener: Learn How to Communicate with Your Dog for Willing Cooperation
**Fennell, J 2004**

Dogspeak: How to Learn It, Speak It and Use It to have a Happy, Healthy Well-Behaved Dog
**Dibra, B, and Crenshaw, M A 1999**

Family-Friendly Dog Training: A Six Week

Program for You and Your Dog
**McConnell, P and Moore, A 2007**

For the Love of a Dog: Understanding Emotion in You and Your Best Friend
**McConnell, P 2007**

How Dogs Think: Understanding the Canine Mind
**Coren, S 2004**

How to Be the Leader of the Pack ... and Have Your Dog Love You for It
**McConnell, P 1996**

How to Speak Dog: Mastering the Art of Dog–Human Communication
**Coren, S 2004**

If Dogs Could Talk: Exploring the Canine Mind
**Csanyi, V, translated by Quandt, R E 2006**

The Intelligence of Dogs: A Guide to the Thoughts, Emotions and Inner Lives of Our Canine Companions
**Coren, S 1995**

On Talking Terms with Dogs: Calming Signals
**Rugaas, T 2005**

Play Together, Stay Together – Happy and Healthy Play Between People and Dogs
**London, K and McConnell, P 2008**

The Other End of the Leash: Why We Do What We Do Around Dogs
**McConnell, P 2003**

Puppy's First Steps: the Whole-Dog Approach to Raising a Happy, Healthy, Well-Behaved Puppy
**Dodman, N H with Lindner, L 2007**

You Are a Dog: Life Through the Eyes of Man's Best Friend
**Bain, T 2004**

# Useful contacts

Listed below are the websites of the major national agencies for welfare, agility, holistic health and breed clubs, plus a few that will be of general interest for dog lovers.

## NATIONAL WELFARE SOCIETIES

American Society for the Prevention of Cruelty to Animals (US)
**aspca.org**

Royal Society for the Prevention of Cruelty to Animals (UK)
**rspca.org.uk**

RSPCA Australia
**rspca.org.au**

## NATIONAL KENNEL CLUBS

American Kennel Club
**akc.org**

The Kennel Club UK
**thekennelclub.org.uk**

Australian National Kennel Council
**ankc.org.au**

## NATIONAL AGILITY ORGANIZATIONS

## AMERICA:

United States Dog Agility Association
**usdaa.com**

## UNITED KINGDOM:

British Agility Association
**baa.uk.net**

The Agility Club
**agilityclub.co.uk**

Agility at the Kennel Club UK
**thekennelclub.org.uk/ agility**

## AUSTRALIA:

Agility Dog Association of Australia
**adaa.com.au**

## INFORMATION ON ALTERNATIVE AND HOLISTIC HEALTH TREATMENTS

American Holistic Veterinary Medical Association
**ahvma.org**

British Association of Holistic Nutrition and Medicine
**bahnm.org.uk**

Holistic Animal Therapy Organisation (Australia)
**hato.com.au**

International Alliance for Animal Therapy and Healing
**iaath.com**

## WEBSITES FOR GENERAL INTEREST

**thebark.com**
A wide-ranging site belonging to US magazine *The Bark*. Lots of posts and articles on many topics, from dog behaviour to dogs and politics.

**theotherendoftheleash. com**
The site of author, behaviourist and trainer Patricia McConnell. An interesting mix of the scholarly (excellent posts on species behaviour) and the personal (lots of photographs of her Border collies and her homestead).

**clickertraining.com**
Site run by Karen Pryor, who first popularized clicker training. Even if you don't use a clicker, it makes good reading.

**hslf.typepad.com**
The site of the Humane Society Legislative Fund, which campaigns politically in the US for the protection of animals. The general interest section, on animals and politics, offers some thought-provoking articles.

# Index

## Author

Sophie Collins is a writer and editor specializing in dog behaviour. Among her previous titles are *Tail Talk: The Secret Language of Dogs* and *Why Does My Dog Do That?*

## Picture Credits

**Getty Images**/Suzanne Opton: 171tr; **Ivan Hissey**: 13, 20, 23, 24, 25, 27; **iStockphoto**: All images other than those specified here; **The Ivy Press**: 101; Photos.com: 138; **Nick Ridley Photography**: 26br, 70br, 71tr, 114, 123b, 125, 127, 128b, 130t, 132b, 133b, 134b, 135bl, 136bl, 148bl, 172b, 185tr.

Quercus Publishing Plc
21 Bloomsbury Square
London
WC1A 2NS

First published in 2010

This edition produced by Ivy Contract

Text by Sophie Collins

A catalogue record of this book is available from the British Library

UK and associated territories
ISBN: 978 1 84866 047 2

USA and associated territories
ISBN: 978 1 84866 074 8

Printed and bound in China

10 9 8 7 6 5 4 3 2 1